TALES OF CYBERCRIME AND OTHER CYBER TALES

TALES OF CYBERCRIME AND OTHER CYBER TALES

Eamon P. Doherty Ph.D.

authorHOUSE®

AuthorHouse™
1663 Liberty Drive
Bloomington, IN 47403
www.authorhouse.com
Phone: 1-800-839-8640

First published by AuthorHouse   05/20/2011

ISBN: 978-1-4634-0204-4 (sc)
ISBN: 978-1-4634-0227-3 (dj)
ISBN: 978-1-4634-0226-6 (ebk)

Library of Congress Control Number: 2011907931

Printed in the United States of America

This book is dedicated to my lovely wife Ester and my wonderful mom, whom my in laws call "Mom D."

Forward and Disclaimer

THIS MANUSCRIPT IS a fictional story with fictional characters. However; the reader may extract digital forensic concepts and security concepts. The ideas and viewpoints expressed by the fictional characters are only in the realm of possibilities to show what some people could be thinking and bring those ideas forward.

The motivation for the book is to take complex and intimidating ideas and present them in an edutainment format so that one can learn and be entertained at the same time. Many college students without technical backgrounds have told me over the years that it would be nice to have a book that introduces Cybercrime concepts in a simplified story format for the busy professional who is juggling the responsibilities of family, work, church, and community events.

Sometimes younger people with children have extended stays in hospitals, may be deployed in the military, or have other reasons that keep them away from their loved ones. Grandparents sometimes then find themselves in changing caregiver roles with grandchildren and computers. I once taught an introductory computer class where a woman introduced herself as an eighty year old grandmother with a new computer and a grandson. She told the class that she needs to quickly understand the dangers of the Internet and needs to learn strategies to help keep him safe online at her home. This book could be read by an eighteen year old high school senior or by an eighty year old person who needs to understand the dangers of the Internet and some of the crimes that exist.

Conversely, this book is also written for those with some interest in computer forensics, cell phone forensics, private investigation, or school administration. There are many legal concepts such as fruit of the poisonous tree, chain of custody, and Fourth Amendment Exception that one will find along with technical concepts blended in an easy to read story format. However; this book is not a legal manual and is not a technical manual but is a story to introduce the reader to concepts that they can explore further elsewhere. The book is broken up into nearly fifty chapters so that one can quickly see an example of a certain concept and find it later. I hope you enjoy the story and learn something too.

Chapter 1

Thanksgiving and GPS

IT WAS THANKSGIVING morning and Grandpa Mike's family came over to his home in the northeast of the USA. Grandpa Mike had inherited the home from his wealthy relatives and now had his family come over for a visit. Grandma Sally had cooked some freshly made butternut squash that she gave everyone at the table. She also had some turkey, mashed potatoes, peas, and cranberry sauce for everyone. Grandpa Mike did not cook any of the dinner but contributed to every holiday with his salty tales of his trucking days.

Dr. Bill was his grandson. He came to the gathering with his Ph.D. and air of superiority that Grandpa Mike did not like. Many other relatives now sat down at the table and were looking forward to another holiday with an interesting exchange of dialogue between Dr. Bill and Grandpa Mike.

Dr. Bill was sitting with his relatives at the table and leaned over as he pulled up a bag. Then he removed a car GPS too which he had used to navigate to the house. He told everyone how great it was and that he was able to pair it with his cell phone using a Bluetooth connection. Grandpa Mike had a car GPS too and listed to his grandson. Dr. Bill said that he often received important phone calls while in the car and could do it hands free. Grandpa Mike said, "What do you do that is so important that it cannot wait until you arrive at your destination?" "Don't you know that talking on the phone can distract you?" Dr. Bill said that he often brainstormed with other academics while driving and since it was hands free, there was no problem.

Grandpa Mike said that he liked Vietnamese food and could often use his GPS to find a Vietnamese restaurant. Then he could use a feature on the GPS to help him drive there after selecting it. Grandpa Mike said, "I can see the number of restaurants in the area and then choose the closest one." Dr. Bill said, "I don't like the location feature too much." "When I visited the Laser Spine Institute near King of Prussia Pennsylvania, I found a postal sorting station and not a post office." Grandpa Mike said the GPS Receiver is pretty good but it still requires a person to make a good choice. "You were the one that chose that from the list, there were many better post office choices to choose from college boy."

Grandpa Mike laughed and said that he was getting forgetful and often needed a GPS for his car. He said, "The other day I walked for an hour at the mall parking lot and pushed the panic button as I walked from row to row." "Then after an hour and some questioning from mall security, we found it." "They drove me around and I pushed the key fob until we heard the horn honking and saw the lights flashing." Dr. Bill then snipped, "Grandpa, if you read your March 2010 issue of your large print Reader's Digest, you would have seen there is a new program called Carfinder that works with your Blackberry." Grandpa Mike said, "Hey college boy, you know I am retired and a bit tight with the bucks." Dr. Bill said, "It is free and is made by Neoistec [1]."

Dr. Bill then said that he also used his Garmin to mark his parking spot as a waypoint. Then he took it with him in case he either forgot where he parked or because the lighting was poor. Grandma Sally asked both of them, "Why can't you just write down the sign on the big pole such as E1 or something such as three rows in front of Macys?"

Grandpa Mike and Dr. Bill and everyone else finished dinner and then sat down on the couch to relax. The couch was actually the bench seat from Grandpa Mike's 18 wheeler that he drove before retiring. He also had a Cobra CB radio mounted next to the couch and frequently spoke to some of his old friends when they were in range on channel 19. Grandpa Mike started to tell of his glory days as a trucker before GPS was used.

Dr. Bill said, "Don't tell me that you quit trucking because of GPS." Grandpa Mike said, "It is true, they put a transponder in my truck and knew how fast I was going and where I stopped." "They also knew how long I slept at the truck pull off on the highway." "Then my friend called Kingfisher got fired when they found out that he got a flat at the same place all the time, coincidentally his girlfriend's house." "I had to drive at a speed I was not comfortable with and found there were no time for bathroom breaks." "In fact in order to make deadlines, I had to wear

"Depends" diapers and then clean up at my destination." In my opinion, the GPS transponders and the computerized maps turned trucking from an enjoyable way of life into some profit maximized business."

Dr. Bill's brother Double D is a detective in New Jersey and then said that he recently solved a murder because of a GPS enabled cell phone. Double D said, "This guy was a suspect for murder since one of his business partners disappeared." "We think it was inspired by the mob because the guy would not sell his share of the flower business and did not want to get in drug trafficking." "Then I questioned the suspect and got a search warrant for his phone." "I used Susteen Secure View with his cell phone and then got some pictures that appeared to be the bloody body and makeshift grave in the swamp." "The pictures had some embedded GPS coordinates in them which I automatically mapped to Google Maps using Susteen's Secure View's Gallery feature." "Then we went to the site and found the body. There were some traces of dirt in the trunk that were the same that were on the victim's shoes." "It was a slam dunk case and the guy is doing time in Rahway or Trenton or somewhere like that."

Dr. Bill then asked, "Why would someone take a picture of a bloody body and makeshift grave?" Double D said, "He needs to show the mob boss that there is proof that the guy is out of the way and the job is done." "In the days of the American Revolution and before, a scalp was taken by the Indians or others as a proof that a person was killed. In history you may have studied the Drummer's War of the 1720s where British colonial authorities offered £100 per Indian scalp.

Grandpa Mike said, "How do you get the information out of the GPS Device." Double D said," You get the GPS device and then connect a cable from it to the computer." "Then you run Paraben's Device Seizure 4.0 and then follow the wizards on screen." "You acquire the data and then use the product to make a report." "Then you must also update the chain of custody form that discusses who has the GPS Device and how and where it was stored for the whole time." Double D then pointed his finger and said, "Make sure the cleaning people cannot get to it after hours and keep that GPS thing locked up!"

Double D's son was home from the military and said to everyone, "Let's have a debriefing." We learned that GPS had some good uses such as helping people find their car, find restaurants and businesses, and could be used to solve some crimes. It could also be used to monitor people and really control their movements when far away. It could be used in many ways that the founders of GPS probably did not intend for the technology to be used.

References

1. Readers Digest, March 2010, Large Print Edition, Page 116-117

Chapter 2

Video Conferencing, Kids and Strangers

GRANDPA MIKE HAD a birthday party and invited all his relatives over. Double D and his son gave grandpa a hearty hug and handshake. Then Dr. Bill came over and hugged everyone too. Then Grandpa Mike's other adult son, Garth, came up from the basement. Garth lives in the basement. He moved there after having a failed career in business. Garth commonly refers to himself as one of the boomerang generation who has left the family and then returned later in life to live in his childhood room again.

Garth said that he was videoconferencing with a woman in Russia. Grandpa Mike asked how he did that. He said that he used his Windows 98 desktop and a built in program called Netmeeting. Grandpa Mike asked, "Garth, why do you use such an old system?" Garth said, "It was free and I found it on garbage night in town." Dr. Bill asked, "Who do you video conference with?" Garth said," I video conference with these Russian and Latvian women that are looking for a western husband." Grandpa Mike said, "You should be careful of the people that you meet and speak to online, because people trafficking is a crime." "Sometimes the person who you are talking to is a man dressed up as a woman and you cannot tell the difference with that low resolution webcam."

Grandpa Mike then walked over and said, "Garth, I forbid you to keep up this fantasy, go and meet the woman you wish to date or marry!" Garth said to him that there was a romance tour to Russia where one can go with many American men to a party and there are eight times as many Russian women there. Grandpa Mike said, "You know nothing about these women and their motives and I don't like it." Grandpa Mike's other grandson Dan is about fifteen and was listening in on the conversation. Dan had his ear on a drinking glass and put the glass on the wall. He heard everything.

Later on that day, Dan said to Garth, "I got Dad's credit card, let's have some fun." Then Garth and Dan got on an adult website and put in Dad's credit card. They were soon doing the online equivalent of a peep show with some women in Russia. Garth did not care that Dan was not eighteen. Double D then came downstairs to get the guys since the football game was coming on TV. Double D realized what happened and said that both men broke the law. Garth was contributing to the corruption of a minor and Dan stole his father's card and made an unauthorized transaction to look at adult material. Double D yelled at both of them and said, "Your dad is going to get all kinds of funny mail and emails and your mom is going to think your father is a pervert." "You have no idea of the harm you did."

Then Garth videoconferenced with some lady from Moldavia and heard about something called the Darknet where people share files. He then downloaded some pictures and videos from the Darknet. Double D did not see Garth watching the game and knew it was too long for a bathroom break. He found Garth downstairs downloading pictures and videos of women. Double D then unplugged Garth's Ethernet connection and said, "How irresponsible are you?" "Many of those kinds of pictures and videos from the Internet are rumored to have malware, spyware, and nasty little viruses in them." "Do you scan what you download or even care where you go online?"

Later on that day, Grandpa Mike was getting some strange phone calls and a heavy breather was talking about some of the activities at their home. Grandpa Mike was outraged and afraid at the same time? He yelled at Garth and Dan and asked how this could have happened.

Double D, Dr. Bill, Grandpa Mike, Garth, and Dan all went downstairs and then noticed that the webcam light went on by itself. When Dan's tape recorder got too close to the microphone by the computer, there was a loud feedback screech. That meant that the microphone was live. Double D said, "There must be a webcam virus and that someone was operating the webcam and microphone without our knowledge." Double D looked at the computer and saw that there was no firewall or spyware or up to date antivirus software. Then he saw that half of the registry was gone and there were no log files on the computer.

Grandpa Mike said," I don't even think that Microsoft supports Windows 98 anymore in 2010." Double D said, "I will move this computer to the living room upstairs, install windows 7, and then get an up to date subscription for security that includes a firewall, antispyware, and antivirus software." Grandpa Mike said that would be a good idea but the stores are closed, let's wait until the next family gathering."

The doorbell rang and a cake soon arrived upstairs. Everyone sang Happy Birthday to Grandpa Mike. He went to blow out the candles and Grandma Sally asked what he wished for. Grandpa Mike said, "I wish people in this family would grow up, get jobs, and stop looking at adult material online." Then Grandpa Mike opened up all his gifts and everyone went home.

Chapter 3

Online Gambling, Video Games, and Poker Teams

GRANDPA MIKE DECIDED to have the family over for the Martin Luther King holiday since everyone had off and it was a national holiday. Everyone watched a movie about a man's addiction and ruin with gambling called, "Owing Mahowney." Soon after, each member of the family had lunch and talked about their daily activities with school and work.

Uncle Robbie had a giant box of assorted video games on video poker. He said that he installed every video poker game he could find and practiced with them until he could regularly win more than he lost. Many of the video poker games had tutorials and you could find out what you did wrong in each hand. Uncle Robbie used all the games as simulators or trainers. Uncle Robbie said, "Let's take these games downstairs." "Garth and Dan, and get ready to win some cash!" Everyone went downstairs and installed all the games. There are so many types of computer software of video poker games, Hoyle Card Games 2008, Slots and Multiplay Video Poker, and lots of others.

Dan said that many adults play online and learn strategy online at places such as *http://www.videopoker.com/*. Dan said playing online was the new way to go but Uncle Robbie said that playing offline on a laptop or desktop was a lot safer until they became experts. Garth said that there was no problem if Grandpa Mike came downstairs since they were only playing offline without using real money.

Dan went upstairs and soon Garth and Uncle Robbie were online playing video poker. They were winning points and doing fine. Then Uncle Robbie decided to go to an online casino and try his luck. Garth said that some online casinos were out of the jurisdiction of the United States and not regulated by the gaming commission. According to

CasinoMeister, many casinos have not paid out, confiscated winnings, or have threatened players [1]. Garth said that it was important to find an online casino that was reputable and governed by a commission. The U.K. and Malta both have websites that have gambling commissions [2],[3]. Both websites have phone numbers and email for people's questions. They soon played some reputable online casinos and won a few hundred dollars on video poker using the strategies they learned on the video games. They learned when to hold them and fold them and when to walk away. They never played impulsively.

The party was soon over and Uncle Robbie asked Garth if he wanted to go on a roadtrip to Atlantic City known as A.C. Garth grabbed his wallet and ran out before Grandpa Mike could say no. They went to the slot machines and won five hundred dollars from a five dollar slot machine. Uncle Robbie said that the 5 dollar machines give the big payouts and it is important to play all three rows at 15 bucks a pull.

Then Uncle Robbie played slot machines that were in full view of the entrances, exits, and walkways to other casinos. Uncle Robbie said, "It is my experience that these machines often payout because they are in full view of the public and casino owners like nothing more than to showcase happy people winning money." "I heard that it does nothing to increase gambling if a person wins in a corner where others cannot see it."

Uncle Robbie and Garth soon had a pile of money using the techniques they learned but then they got greedy and played impulsively and lost it all except the $100 that Uncle Robbie put in his shoe. Garth was so upset. Then Uncle Robbie said, "We came in with $100 and we left with $100. We had fun. It is time to go home.

On the way home, they stopped at White Castle and got a bag of hamburgers and large diet sodas and some onion rings. Then Grandpa Mike's dog heard the car pull up and started barking. The lights went on and Grandpa Mike opened the door and started yelling. His neighbors woke up and turned their lights on too. Everyone heard the yelling as Garth came back into the house.

Then Uncle Robbie brought in some packages from the car and went downstairs to comfort Garth. Uncle Robbie said, "We could go to an online poker site." "You, me, and Dan could work as a team and pass cards to each other." "We could pretend that we are new to card playing and our mistakes would be perceived as naiveté and not teamwork." "We could all sit next to each other with laptops, see each other's hands, and then pass each other the cards we need." "I could use my old computer with a modem and dial into AOL in Arizona and make it look like I was in Arizona." "Dan could use my other old laptop with a modem and dial into an ISP in Arkansas and look like he is there." "We could all be in the same room but appear to be spread around the country."

Garth said, "Uncle Robbie, that is illegal and we would get caught." "Didn't you know there is software to catch poker teams and poker bots and Trojans?" Haven't you heard of Poker Bodyguard 1.0 or Havana Catch Download?" Uncle Robbie said, "It is getting harder to cheat with all this new technology, guess we better keep our day jobs and stay honest." Then Uncle Robbie went home.

References

1. Owing Mahowney, VHS Format, Sony Pictures Classics, ISBN 1-4049-2281-4
2. URL Accessed on December 28, 2010 *http://www.casinomeister. com/rogue/#rogue*
3. URL Accessed on December 28, 2010 *www.gamblingcommission. gov.uk*
4. URL Accessed on December 28, 2010 *http://www.lga.org.mt/ lga/home.aspx*
5. URL Accessed on December 28, 2010 *http://www.soft32download. com/software/Poker-BodyGuard-download-details.html*

Chapter 4

Chatrooms, IM, and Sexual Predators

GRANDPA MIKE WAS in the living room with Grandma Sally and Aunt Mary. Aunt Mary moved in with them ten years ago and was only going to stay for a year but it seems like she moved in for good. Aunt Mary does not say too much and never helps with the dishes but does let the dog out. Aunt Mary was having a birthday and asked that all the family come over to celebrate. Everyone watches "Uncle Buck" with John Candy. The neighborhood young adults also came over because everyone likes Aunt Mary who is like a big kid too.

Then Garth and Dan and some of the neighborhood kids go downstairs and use the computer. They go into the chatroom and start talking to people. They are unsupervised and soon go into some adult chatrooms about various sexual fetishes. The guys laughed as they made up some dialogue and played along with some of the racy conversations. Then Dan realized that his profile was still public and still displayed his address and phone number for anyone to see. His cell phone was ringing and various people called him and said some unsettling things. What started out as a prank soon became a nightmare. Dan used Grandpa Mike's home address in his online profile and soon there were some really strange characters and cars cruising in front of Grandpa Mike's house.

Grandpa Mike yelled downstairs for everyone to get upstairs! Then he said, "I cannot leave you guys alone online without supervising you!" "That darn computer causes more grief than all the other problems combined in this house." "I am getting Double D over here to see what he can do to stop this and control the situation at our home."

Double D then came over and Grandpa Mike explained the problem. Double D said that the computer needs to come up to the living room and there needs to be some responsible adult supervision. Double D also said that there should be no expectation of privacy policy explained to everyone in the house. Then he said, "I could install various

11

programs from Spectorsoft that allow you to easily see all the chatroom conversations, email, and other activities online [1]." "We could playback websites visited, chats, and other things too."

Double D then installed eBlaster and Spectorsoft on the computers and Grandpa Mike gave him permission to remotely monitor the computer's activity from his home since Grandpa Mike was more interested in watching TV and reading the newspaper. Double D installed everything and then set it so he could view it remotely from his home and see what Dan or Garth was doing online.

Once Double D installed the software and explained the lack of privacy issue, everyone behaved for a while.

References

1. URL accessed December 28,2010 *http://www.spectorsoft.com/*

Chapter 5

Keyloggers, Hardware and Software

GRANDPA MIKE CALLED up Double D because he got his credit card bill and saw there was about thirty charges for things he never ordered. There was women's lingerie, a trip to A.C., and lots of adult novelty items. Double D laughed because all these items were out of character for Grandpa Mike to purchase. He asked how this credit card fraud could have happened and how someone could have taken all his credit card numbers and passwords.

After a while, Double D checked the computer and saw that there was an unknown adapter between the keyboard and the desktop computer. After careful examination, he saw it was a hardware keylogger. It recorded every keystroke that Grandpa Mike typed in. It seemed that someone who visited the house placed it there and came back later for it and dumped the data. This connector went in a PS/2 port in the back of the computer.

Double D suggested putting a hidden camera in the house and then recording it on the VCR for playback. Grandpa Mike asked, "How could we do that and would it be expensive?" Double D said he had a clock with a camera hidden in the 2 and it costs under one hundred dollars. There are clocks with hidden cameras in them. We could also use a clock with a wireless camera and connect it to a receiver that could go to a computer or DVR to record it [1].

Life went on and then the fraud continued to happen with the checking account too. Double D came over and went through the video on the computer. He saw that it was one of the neighbor's children who removed the keylogger and put it back later. Double D said, "At this point we go to the police with everything and it becomes a criminal matter. "It is the Silver Platter Doctrine and now the 4th Amendment comes into play."

Double D calls the police and they arrive. Double D explains the situation, gives them the credit card receipts, the bank statements, and the video. The police say they will review the evidence and issue a warrant if necessary.

References

1. URL Accessed December 28, 2010 http://www.paramountzone. com/clock-spy-camera.htm

Chapter 6

Eavesdropping on the Phone

GRANDPA MIKE SAID to Aunt Mary and Grandma Sally that he felt someone was listening to his calls and harassing him online and on the phone. Aunt Mary was such a good listener. She sat on the couch day after day and watched everyone. She was almost invisible to everyone but now she spoke up and offered some advice. Aunt Mary said, "I think that the neighbor's son was at the side of our house and connected his phone to the open jack in our NID box that connects to the phone." "You know that I sit here day after day and look out the window and at the TV." "I see everything that goes on in this house and nobody talks to me about it."

Grandma Sally said, "I saw one of his friends with him holding a Butt Set." Aunt Mary asked what is a Butt Set? Grandma Sally said, "It looks like an orange telephone handset with two wires and metal clips."

Garth came upstairs a little while ago and heard everything. He then said to the group upstairs on the couch in the living room that it might have been eavesdropping on our new IP Phone. "The IP phone is the phone that connects to the computer router." "I feel that the neighbor's kids may have connected to our router wirelessly since we have no security and then while connected, they eavesdropped on the phone." Aunt Mary asked if that was difficult. Garth said, "All they needed to do was run a program to collect packets while connected to our network and collect and reassemble our packets." Aunt Mary stood up in her sweatsuit and went to get another Ritz cracker with peanut butter on top. Garth said, "I saw a Youtube video of Netwitness at Blackhat 2010 that showed it is possible to use Netwitness to rebuild captured packets from a voice over IP conversation and then listen in on."

Grandpa Mike said that he got some weird calls at 2 AM and then some strange people came knocking on the door at 3 AM. Double D came over and put a lock on the NID box and added some security, including encryption to their router to try to stop them.

Grandma Sally said, "It is a shame that such good products like Netwitness which are law enforcement tools can potentially be abused by criminals or mischievous kids for bad purposes." Grandpa Mike said, "A screwdriver can be used to fix a broken item and help people or it can be a burglar tool." "It all depends on the intent of the person using the tool." "I remember seeing a commercial that said guns don't kill people, people kill people."

References

1. URL Accessed 4/26/2011 http://www.wireshark.org/about.html

Chapter 7

HIPAA, Hospitals, WebTV

GRANDPA MIKE WAS home and eating pork rinds, fried eggs, and a beer while sitting in his easy chair. He felt dizzy, had some chest pains, and slid to the floor. When he woke up, he was in the hospital with tubes in his body and lots of wires connected to him. He was also on a heart catheter device with a monitor nearby. The doctor said to Grandpa Mike, you sure should thank God that Garth is AED CPR certified and restarted the electrical patterns correctly with your heart. He gave you CPR, pulled off your shirt, placed the pads on your chest, and then pushed the button to give you a jolt. He then called 911 and we got you here immediately.

Grandpa Mike said, "I want to email my friends and send them a request to pray for me to get better." "Can I have my laptop from home?" The doctor said, "No way Mike, you are not going to connect to our networks with an unknown laptop." "We have protected health care information on it and your access could potentially be a HIPAA violation if you have malware that starts collecting and sending protected health care information out." Grandpa Mike, "What is HIPAA?" The doctor and the nurse who walked in explained that HIPAA was a 1996 law enacted by President Clinton to protect the patients from people who misuse information. [1]"

Grandpa Mike said, "Yes of course, HIPAA is a good law and its effects are good." "I remember having erectile dysfunction in the early 1990s and then getting all this embarrassing mail delivered to my home." "Once my neighbor came over to my house with junk mail for a penis pump with my name on it and laughed." "With HIPAA, my medical condition data is not marketed to everyone."

The Doctor then said, "Privacy is not protected so much back in my home country in the Far East." "The USA may take privacy too far sometimes but overall it is very good." "Grandpa Mike, I will arrange for you to get WebTV so you can surf the web and do email from the hospital." "Next year, our IT department is going to arrange for a non secured web access area for guests so patients can bring their laptop and connect to the network." "You can call me Dr. Raj."

The nurse came in with the WebTV keyboard and had the account set up. Doctor Raj said, "WebTV is good because we don't get the malware, spyware, and viruses on our computers and patients can still do email with people." "It really frees our IT from many of the security issues that are present when non employees surf the web, watch videos, and do email."

Grandpa Mike said, "Some of my relatives might come to the hospital and then bring their laptops and connect to whatever unsecured network is in range of the hospital." "My son's laptop has a tools feature that displays a map of all the local wireless networks, their strength, and if they are secured." Dr. Raj said, "I believe it is not lawful to connect to other's networks without permission." Grandpa Mike said, "If it is not documented and enforced, who cares?"

Dr. Raj said, "Some people have told me that they like WebTV because they cannot afford a computer, yet with Web TV they can still do email and surf the web." "Web TV helps break down the digital divide that separates those with money and online access, from those without online access and home computers to benefitting from the information highway."

"The world has come a long way." "In 2000, Secretary General Kofi Anon said that half the world never made a phone call. [2]" "Now I read that approximately half of humanity has a cell phone, much of it with Internet connectivity." "That also means that we can call each other, help each other, email each other, or do Cybercrimes to each other, it is our choice how to act."

Dr. Raj then said to Grandpa Mike," If your vitals are good and you keep up the recovery, you can go home in three days."

References

1. Maiwald, E., (2003), "Network Security, A Beginner's Guide", second edition, McGraw Hill Publishing, California, USA, p107,
2. URL Accessed 4/16/2011 http://www.shirky.com/writings/half_the_world.html

Chapter 8

Nannycams and Abuse

G RANDPA MIKE WAS back home and using a Zimmer Frame to get around. Sometimes he needed help and had some trouble speaking or remembering things. Aunt Mary, Grandma Sally, and some of the other people usually around went on a spiritual retreat nearby to recover from all the recent stress and to pray for Grandpa Mike. Garth was busy with day trading and doing his computer activities downstairs and did not have the patience to be a health care aide, even for his closest of relatives. Garth let everyone know that it is one thing to do CPR and AED on someone but quite another to spend all day everyday caring for someone.

The family could not afford a regular nurse and the health insurance they had did not cover a home aide. Garth solved the problem by getting day laborers from downtown. He would cruise by the train station in the family car and roll down the window. He would often pick out one of the cute immigrant women and bring her home to take care of Grandpa Mike. At the end of the day she got a $100 cash. There were no papers, no interviews, and he did not even know if they were legal immigrants."

Grandpa Mike sometimes yelled when the home care person improperly lifted him. Then he would whimper for a while. The woman got angry when his noise interfered with her TV shows. She hit him hard twice and once she put her cigarette butt out on his hand.

Grandpa Mike called up Double D and explained the situation to him. Grandpa Mike said, "I am getting some elder abuse." "I cannot afford a real nurse so I get these day laborers in to take care of me." "I cannot complain because I need them but the abuse is awful." "Can you help me catch their abuse and record it so we can prosecute them or at least show others not to use that person's services again." "I also want to show the family that this stuff goes on." "The laborers act so nice to others and say it is me burning my hand on the stove and not their cigarette." "These women put on this miss sweet little thing act and everyone thinks I am a liar or a crazy old man."

Double D came over to the house with a Teddy Bear. Grandpa Mike liked it and hugged it. It was big, white, soft and it had a wireless camera in it that connected to a receiver. The receiver was connected to a TV and VCR in another room. The VCR was in SLP mode or super long playing mode which allowed six hours of recording. The bear and the transmitter and receiver only cost $65.00 with shipping. It was from a Chinese mom and pop company in San Francisco and the kit was made in the People's Republic of China.

Soon Grandpa Mike felt better. He held the bear and the eyes of the bear faced the aide. One eye was a camera while one eye was not. However; you could not tell the difference. The bear used a nine volt battery and transmitted on either channel A,B,C, or D on the 2.4 Gigahertz frequency. Double D put the bear on channel D so that it did not interfere with the wireless cordless phone or the Internet router in the house. Channel C could not be used since the house next store had a baby monitor that used that frequency. Double D could easily check in on the neighbor's baby by moving the receiver to channel C.

Soon, one of the day laborers started smacking Grandpa Mike and verbally abusing him. Then she phoned up her boyfriend who came over and they were having sex on the couch. She looked about 25 but the guy looked about 17. Grandpa Mike called up Double D and explained everything. The whole thing was on tape. Then Double D saw the evidence. He phoned up the local police who had jurisdiction in that area and now it became a criminal investigation.

The police soon came over and took a statement from Grandpa Mike. Then they took many pictures of the house and sketched things. The older policeman told the rookie policemen that the picture numbers will correspond to the sketches in the house and it will help with the report later. Then they filled out a chain of custody form and bagged and tagged the evidence which included the: bear, the TV, the VCR, and the tapes. These items were all taken into evidence and they might be returned sometime after court.

References

1. Graham, B, McGowan, K., (2006), "101 Spy Gadgets for the Evil Genius", Tab electronics, Macgraw Hill companies, NY, NY, Project 33 classic Nanny Cam, Page 72

Chapter 9

Reverse Lookup for Cell Phone Numbers and Email Addresses

GARTH NEEDED SOME money since he lost too much at day trading. He decided to sell things at the many flea markets around. A friend of his told him to go to New York City and park by this fire hydrant a few blocks away from the Holland Tunnel. Garth used the family vehicle and drove over there. A man knew what kind of car Garth had and was expecting him. Garth parked the vehicle by the fire hydrant and stood there. The man approached him and told him not to worry about parking there, it was arranged with the police that no ticket would be issued. Garth thought to himself that the man was lying because how could one get the police not to ticket a car in front of a fire hydrant?

They went inside the storefront which looked like a bar. Garth thought they might have a drink and talk about business but upon closer inspection he could see the bottles were empty and the bar was fake. Garth said, "Hey, what kind of place is this?" The man pushed the wall and the entire door was a revolving door which went into a large warehouse. There were all kinds of people working there. It was unbelievable that such an operation could exist in New York City. Garth bought loads of consumer electronics and watches that looked like designer products yet he suspected they were not. Garth said, "Wow, Rolllex watches !" "Hmm is there three Ls in Rolex?" Everything was done in cash.

Then Garth said he was done and wondered how to get out? There appeared to be no door, just walls and no windows. Then the man pushed part of the wall and they were back in the fake bar. Garth saw a phone number on a piece of paper on the floor and scooped it up. Then he left and drove home.

Garth went up to Grandpa Mike and the newest aide and said here is a bonus, a Rolllex watch. He instructed them to learn to use the features and see how reliable it was. Within the first hour of wearing it, the crown above the word Rolllex fell off and was moving around in the watch. This new aide was polite and offered to take the watch apart and glue the crown back in place for Grandpa Mike.

Grandpa Mike noticed the paper with the phone number fall out of Garth's pocket when he pulled his keys out. Grandpa Mike asked who it belonged to. Garth did not know. Grandpa Mike said that he heard from a friend that if you go to *www.spokeo.com*, there is an option to look up email addresses, phone numbers, and if you have a phone number, it will tell you who it belongs to. Garth looked up the number later and found it was not registered to anyone. He thought it was one of those disposable cell phones you can buy at the convenience store for cash and do not have to register.

Garth said, "Did you know that when people buy those phones, they always scan the package when you leave." "That means that the phone, the store, and the time of purchase is known." "Did you also know that nearly every convenience store has a camera and digital video recorder because of all the robberies?" "That means that they can link the sale to a person." Grandpa Mike said, "How about if you bought the phone with a credit card or filled out the rebate so they can mail ten bucks to your home?" They both laughed at the anonymity and thought it was only anonymous if you stole it. The time cards for the phone could have been bought with cash but they might be activated from a person's home computer thus establishing a link from the number to the person.

Grandpa Mike and Garth had a talk about the flea markets. Grandpa Mike said, "I used to be known as the sock king." "If you go to this certain address, knock five times at the door and they will open up the garage door and you pull in." "This Chinese lady will sell you all the socks you want cheap for cash. "There were a lot of girls crowded in this hot room full of sewing machines making socks."

Grandpa Mike said, "Years back I made some money by telling all my neighbors that I was into recycling and saving the environment." "They could tie up their newspapers and leave them in my van in front of the house." Then once a week my friend Bob the Bowler would borrow my truck." "I said ok, as long as he dropped off the papers at the recycling center and gave me the money." "I did the same with aluminum cans."

"When the towns got into municipal recycling, it really wrecked my racket."

Garth said," I am also getting into picking up Bar-B-Que grills on garbage day and then bringing them home." "Then I hit the grill with a hammer and knock off all the non aluminum stuff and take it up to the scrap dealer." Grandpa Mike said, "Please be careful about who you meet at the scrap dealer, there are guys that collect miles of copper wire from the railroad and abandoned phone lines." "Some phone lines are in desolate places and extend to rural areas." "That is not their property to sell to the scrap dealers and they are wrong [1]."

Grandpa Mike said, "Garth, I am glad we had this talk, I feel we are closer as a family now."

References

1. Liesik, Geoff, Deseret News, October 27,2010 *http://www.deseretnews.com/article/700076777/3-charged-with-stealing-20-miles-of-copper-wire-from-telephone-poles.html*
2. URL Accessed 12/30/2010, Channel 7 News in Sarasota, Florida, Reported by Monica Buchannan *http://www.youtube.com/watch?v=dE70GdDaGkE*

Chapter 10

Cell Phone Forensics and the Police

DOUBLE D CAME over to Grandpa Mike's house since it was Aunt Mary's birthday. Aunt Mary had an ice cream cake delivered to herself and called many people to come over. She wanted some attention and was tired of being "invisible." Double D, Grandpa Mike, Grandma Sally, Garth, Dr. Bill, and some others came to the dining room of the house where Aunt Mary sits and watches TV all day. Aunt Mary asked someone to sing "Happy Birthday." She then got her wish by blowing out the candles.

Dr. Bill immediately started talking about himself and all his troubles. Then he started giving advice. He said, "Double D, you ought to apply for a grant for a cell phone forensics kit, some additional training, and then be the cell phone forensics offer for your department." "I think some of the grants may pay you for a stipend for the next two years too." Double D said," You are right Dr. Bill, I could get the grant, get a little more salary, and buy the tools." "However; when the grant is up, I will probably go back to my old salary and have the same cell phone forensics duties to do." "Then I will have to argue with the chief and town to pay for new forensics software and cables since the license will be up." "They will not want to hear that the license is up in two years and that we need to buy it again."

Dr. Bill said," Why do you have only two years with the software?" Double D said, "Developers such as Paraben or Susteen or others have tremendous developing costs." "They have to purchase each phone themselves, then figure out the operating system, and then how to do the programming for their tools so they get all the data." "Then they have to validate the tools with the test plan." "Engineers, lawyers, technicians, and programmers all need salaries and health benefits." "Do you realize how many forensic software kits they have to sell just to break even?" "Do you even care?" Dr. Bill said, "You know Double D, as a doctor of technical skills, I tend to only look at the technical things and not at the whole picture." "You are right Double D."

Double D then said, "If I got the cell phone forensics grant, my fellow officers might also be jealous I got the grant, am learning a valuable skill, and am now making more money than they earn." "It could cause frictions in my relations with my peers." "Then when the grant is over, they will say I have more work to do and am not getting paid, it will set a bad precedent with the police union." "They will not like me going to a lesser salary and then having more work to do."

Dr. Bill said, "Do you think that you could get the grant and then when it is over, change careers?" Double D said, "If I don't stay in the police department for twenty-five years, then I lose my health benefits for life." Dr. Bill said, "Why don't you go for a grant when you are ready to retire and make a career change?" Double D said, "That is what I will do."

Dr. Bill said, "I think that I will learn cell phone forensics more and get my CCE, certified computer examiner certification." "Then I will get my cell phone forensics certificates from Paraben, Susteen, and a few other private education providers." "Then I will work one day a week for a divorce lawyer extracting pictures and sexting from the phones and preparing them for divorce court." Double D said," There is a lot of that kind of work, remember the Tiger Woods case [1]?

Double D said," You can be famous if you investigate a case where the sports figures allegedly take inappropriate pictures of themselves and email them to others." "Football quarterback Bret Favre was fined $50,000.00 for allegedly sending below the belt photos to Jenn Stenger [2]." Dr. Bill said there is so much alleged sexting this days that I will have plenty of work." "The economy may be down but the number of alleged online misbehaviors are steadily rising."

References

1. Gerdaman, Dina, "TEXTUAL INFIDELITY: The Tiger Woods scandal has sent a message to wives and girlfriends", For The Patriot Ledger, Posted Dec 16, 2009 @ 11:31 AM URL Accessed January 1,2011 *http://www.patriotledger.com/lifestyle/*

x985678274/TEXTUAL-INFIDELITY-The-Tiger-Woods-scandal-has-sent-a-message-to-wives-and-girlfriends

2. URL Accessed January 1, 2011 *http://www.huffingtonpost.com/2010/12/29/brett-favre-fined-sexts_n_802287.html*, Cambell, Dave, The Huffington Post Newspaper published Dec. 29,2010

Chapter 11

Baby Monitors and War Driving

A UNT MARY'S FRIENDS from China stopped by and asked if they could stay a few days. Grandpa Mike proof read some of their papers since they are graduate students at the local university. Aunt Mary said that they could leave their furniture and belongings here until they find a new apartment. Grandpa Mike said, "Their baby is upstairs with a baby monitor on him while Aunt Mary and the parents speak in the kitchen." "Garth saw the baby monitor and asked, "What is the difference between a teddy bear cam / nanny cam and a baby monitor?" Aunt Mary said, "The baby monitor collects sound and video while the teddy bear camera / nanny cam only collects video." "We also have the Sharper Image baby monitor that works on channel A,B,C, or D on 2.4 Gigahertz. It also has a night monitor setting that uses infrared and works in the dark.

The couple said, "Leaving the baby upstairs by himself for a few minutes is possible since we have the baby monitor." "If there is a problem, we will know it and fly like the wind to assist our son and keep him from danger." Garth said, "That sounds good but I am concerned about kidnapping, because people sometimes do wardriving and might learn of your baby." The couple said, "What is wardriving?" Garth said, it is when people drive slowly with a laptop or wireless handheld device and then see what networks that they can connect to or what video camera that they can access [1]."

The people who find the open access networks will also sometimes mark the results of any of these unsecured networks with special symbols on the street so others can find them. They may also mark the download speed or bandwidth for others too [2]. This is called warchalking. It is bad because others may do illegal activities on the network and it looks as if the owner of the network is guilty. Some bad people will use open access networks to exchange child pornography.

Aunt Mary said to people at the birthday party, "I just learned to use the open access computer upstairs and surf the net." I was looking at paints and was thinking about repainting the living room." "Then I saw an article about an additive for paint that uses bits of copper and aluminum so that the wireless network stays only within that room [3]." It was one of the best contributions I could make to this house, security and redecorating at the same time."

Grandpa Mike said that one of his military buddies called him up and was talking about Vietnam and then other topics from bowling to home computers. Grandpa Mike said that his friend Henry got some special computer equipment when they had a surplus sale at the military base. They sold him some Tempest Equipment that did not give off any signals since it was so well shielded [4]. Tempest equipment is made so that people cannot easily eavesdrop on any wireless signals.

Aunt Mary said that was amazing how we were all talking about security and electronics and computers so much in our daily lives. Garth said, "I agree Aunt Mary, my computer and printer and digital camera are so much part of my daily life." "I email people my pictures, talk to new people all the time, and live on the computer at times playing games like network Doom and Everquest."

References

1. URL Accessed 4/16/2011 *http://www.wardriving.com/about.php* Definition of War Driving by Pete Shipley
2. URL Accessed 4/16/2011 *http://www.wordspy.com/words/ warchalking.asp* Definition of Warchalking
3. Lee, D.,(2009), "Anti-wifi Paint Offers Security", BBC News, September 30, 2009, URL http://news.bbc.co.uk/2/hi/8279549. stm

Chapter 12

Virtual Marriage and Bigamy

G RANDPA MIKE FELT much better and no day laborers had come to the house in two days now to take care of him. He felt strong enough to go down a flight of stairs. He had to go downstairs to flip a switch because Aunt Mary ran too many electrical items at once on one outlet. She had an extension cord plugged in and the power strip had an electric heater, a computer, and the TV all running at the same time. Grandpa Mike had not been down there in a while and he was surprised at what he saw. Garth had a stalker shrine [1]. There were all these pictures of his ex-girlfriend glued to this board. Her name was Rachel. Then after she broke up, there were telephoto shots of her up there too. Some of the telephoto shots were altered crudely with scissors or with a photo editor to remove her new boyfriend. There must have been a hundred photos of Rachel on the board.

Grandpa Mike also saw a notebook about his new activities online in a game called Second something. It could have been Second Life. In this virtual world he was married and there was a lady named Mabel who was his virtual wife. Apparently in the virtual world's you can have your avatar or animated person marry another avatar. The notes said that his first online wife refused to change her looks to match his real life ex-girlfriend Rachel. However; even though they were still married, he married this other woman named Rachel and got his new online wife to change her looks so they are the same as his ex-girlfriend in the shrine.

Grandpa Mike realized that there are no laws against virtual bigamy and there is no penalty if Garth gets a virtual divorce. However; it is really creepy. Grandpa Mike was really shattered by this and did not know how he was going to talk to Garth or anyone else in the family about it.

Grandpa Mike asked his old military buddy about it and he said that he heard of a magazine called Cyberpsychology, Behavior, and Social Networking [2]. His military buddy said, "Mike, maybe it is just a phase that Garth is going through and you should not worry about it." Then Grandpa Mike said, "Maybe I should contact some mental health professionals from the journal and see what they think since I am no expert and it might be some warning sign."

Aunt Mary said that she heard about virtual worlds from Garth and it might give her a new outlet on life if she goes online instead of just sitting there every day and watching television. Aunt Mary said, "I might do it, since I could pretend to be anyone I want to be online." "I could be a scientist, or a real estate salesman, or a mayor of a town." Grandpa Mike sighed and thought, "What should I do?" "Should I worry?"

References

1. URL Accessed 4/16/2011 http://tvtropes.org/pmwiki/pmwiki.php/Main/StalkerShrine
2. Cyberpsychology, Behavior, and Social Networking, URL Accessed 4/16/2011 *http://www.mindmodulations.com/mindmods/feeds/17*

Chapter 13

409 Scams

G RANDPA MIKE WAS feeling better and dismissed the daily day workers who used to come to the house. He told Garth to keep these people away. Aunt Mary jumped for joy out of her seat and said, "I just won the Canadian Lottery for a lot of money [1]." Grandpa Mike asked, "When did you purchase Canadian Lottery tickets?" Aunt Mary said, "I did not buy any tickets but maybe someone in Canada bought one for me." Grandpa Mike said, "This sounds bad, I am calling Double D."

Double D arrived at the house and said that people often get scammed about the Canadian Lottery and Saddam Hussein's money. Aunt Mary said, "Tell me about the lottery." Double D said, "A person often calls or emails relentlessly and says you are the winner and you just need to send a fee to a certain place for processing." "Then the person sends the big fee and is never contacted again and never receives any prize."

Aunt Mary said, "Tell me about the Saddam Hussein scam." A person who claims to be an American soldier often says that he captured Saddam Hussein and his money and wants to split it with you." "He asks for a bank account to deposit the money into." However; he never deposits anything but only removes your wealth." This is also known as a 409 or 419 scam.

Aunt Mary then said, "Oh I guess that Nigerian Prince who contacted me and wants to leave Nigeria with his money does not want to share it with me but only take my money." Everyone in the living room had a good laugh. Aunt Mary said, "Guess I will be living here a lot more years !"

Double D said to everyone that 409 or 419 scams require a person to give a bank account number to another person to put money into but in truth they only take money out. There is a website with a map that shows you where in the world most of these scams originate from [2]. The map cannot show that the root of these scams originate from people's greed worldwide. Double D said, "Guys and gals, if it sounds too good to be true, it isn't."

Aunt Mary said, "I guess I will have to earn some money the old fashioned way, by working." "I also include day trading as working." Everyone sighed and threw up their hands.

References

1. URL Accessed 1/1/2011 http://phoenix.about.com/cs/seniors/a/canadianlottery.htm
2. URL Accessed 1/1/2010 http://www.419eater.com/scamtracker/

Chapter 14

Misappropriation of Property

GRANDPA MIKE WAS feeling better. He went fishing in a Johnboat with his old military buddy to a place called the Delaware River. They had a great time and caught some large Muskies. They went back to Grandpa Mike's house and cooked them. Aunt Mary, Garth, Grandma Sally, and some neighbors all had some fish and corn. The two men had a lot of stories about fishing and told everyone how much they enjoyed fishing.

Aunt Mary thought that she might like to have a Johnboat and go fishing in the local lake for bass. There were plenty of weeds and there was a lot of talk about a twelve pound bass that people saw around the cove. She decided that she would buy a Johnboat too.

She saw a Johnboat on an online auction site. She put in a bid and won it. She paid for it. Then she went to the guy's house to pick up the boat. There were ten others at the house who came for the boat. The first sale was legal but the same boat was sold nine more times. Everyone came to the apartment building and tried to grab the boat claiming that they bought it. Each person had a receipt. Another car pulled up and the people said, "I am here for my boat." Nobody answered at the front door of the apartment where the seller lived. Then the building manager said that the man who lived in that apartment moved last night and gave no forwarding address.

The people explained what happened and the building manager called the police. The police came by and then took statements from everyone and made a report. The policeman said that the legal terminology for this type of crime was misappropriation of property [1]. It is ok to sell an item once but once the first sale is made, the seller is not free to sell it again. The other sales following the first one are fraudulent.

The policeman said that he used to work for a private investigator before he became a policeman and that his specialty was "skip trace."

Skip trace is when you use the online resources to see where a person went to after disappearing. His private investigator boss gave him $75 per person that he found. The policeman told the crowd it was hard work and one day he did 5 skip traces. He said, "We should be able to locate him and then we will call you."

References

1. URL Accessed 4/16/2011 Misappropriation of Property, http://law.justia.com/cfr/title36/36-1.0.1.1.2.0.1.20.html

Chapter 15

The Need for Internet and Computer Usage Policies

GARTH APPLIED FOR a job at a local car salesman business and interviewed on the phone for it and got it. Then he showed up for work. There was a desk, a phone, and a computer. There was not too much to do so there was lots of free time.

Garth came in and had a cup of coffee. Then he read the newspaper and shopped for gifts online. Then he did some day trading and saw how his portfolio was doing. Next he did some personal calls and personal email. About two hours later he was ready for work but looked quite busy. This went on for months.

One day the manager saw Garth playing an online version of Solitaire and said, "What the hell are we paying you for Garth?" Garth said, "I sometimes sell cars and call up customers but I have a lot of down time so I do other things." The manager said, "You were playing video games!" Garth said, "I was practicing my hand eye coordination with this laptop." "You gave me a laptop with a trackpoint and the best way for me to get used to it was to play Solitaire." The manager said, "That is either a valid excuse or the best line of bull I ever heard." "No wonder you are such a good salesman."

Another day the manager caught Garth looking at fishing poles and purchasing one. He said, "I caught you buying stuff for your personal life online and that has got nothing to do with work." Garth said, "Yeah, so !" The manager said, "You think we pay you to sit and buy fishing poles so you and your dad can go fishing?" Garth said," When you hired me, you did not say what the computer is for and in fact I really do not need it for work very often." "You also did not have me sign any kind of policy and there is no banner on the computer when I turn it on saying what I can or cannot do." The manager said, "I guess I should have an Internet Usage Policy and a computer usage policy and spell out what can and cannot be done by employees with these machines." Garth said, "You better do that and make sure that your new policies are legal and approved by your general counsel too."

Then the manager had Garth sign these policies and file them with personnel. The manager felt really good about this and then saw Garth playing video games again. He ran up and said, "I caught you and I think I can get you fired now lazy bones." Garth called his lawyer and spoke for a minute. Then Garth said, "Did everyone else with the same position also sign a policy or just me?" The manager got really scared and said, "Just you." Garth said, "It was not equally enforced and if you fire me, I may sue you personally as well as the company and win!"

The manager then made all the other employees sign the same policies and filed them with personnel. He then equally enforced all of them too. This time he would be ready to catch Garth and fire him. It was a bit of a game and Garth never got caught doing any of these bad things. He was so careful and now it was personal between the two of them.

Then one day Garth had a naked person screen saver on the desktop and was caught cruising adult websites. The manager said you not only violated the Internet policy by cruising adult websites but you installed a naked person screen saver which violates the computer usage policy. Then on top of that, you created a hostile workplace with the naked picture screen saver that often appears after two minutes of inactivity.

Garth said, "Ok, I am fired, now I have twenty six weeks of paid unemployment." "Thanks, see you." "By the way, if you need a good read about IT Ethics, the need for policies, and some anecdotes about video games, Stephen Northcutt writes a really nice book on the subject [1]."

References

1. Northcutt, S. (2004)," IT Ethics Handbook: Right and Wrong for IT Professionals", Published by Syngress Books, ISBN 9781931836142

Chapter 16

Counterfeiting and Imaging a suspect's Drive with the Logic Cube

D R. BILL'S SON was at Harvard Medical and the bills were heavy. His wife loved to shop online and Dr. Bill lost a little too much with the online casinos. He needed to make some online money quick. Dr. Bill said that selling coins would be the best way to go. Dr. Bill learned that Morgan silver dollars were a hot item and he had a good collection minus the key coins such as the 1894 or 1895. He bought both coins at online auction places for about five dollars. They were quote hobby coins made in China. Then he sold his complete set online. This was fraud because he represented the entire set as real and did not say the key dates were copies.

Dr. Bill also bought some Confederate States of America (CSA) replica currency notes and mixed them with his real notes. This was fraud because he passed off the entire set as real. He did the same with his CSA savings bonds.

Lastly he scanned some hundred dollar bills and printed them out on a high resolution color laser printer. Then he passed these notes off at busy sporting events and at busy gas stations. This too was fraud.

Dr. Bill got caught because the Secret Service was given the fake notes. They were able to put the notes up to an ultraviolet light and then with the aid of a magnifying glass, see the embedded printer serial number. Dr. Bill was also seen by the Secret Service on the gas station's security camera and digital video recorder passing the notes to the gas attendant. They had him passing the notes to the attendant and his printer serial number too.

The Secret Service came to Dr. Bill's house and arrested him. They got a warrant from a judge and seized his computer. They entered it into a chain of custody. They bagged and tagged it with a bar code. The agents made sure the chain of custody form was good and included everything.

Later the Secret Service imaged the hard drive or cloned it with a device such as the Logic Cube. Then he had an exact copy of the machine's hard drive including the unused space. The unused space often holds swapped data from virtual memory. Then he made sure the drives were equal with the hash marks.

Next the examiner used the Access Data's FTK, forensic toolkit and recovered the temp files with the transactions of selling the fraudulent coin sets. They also had his transactions of the purchasing of the replica coins. Lastly, the log file showed that he printed the counterfeit paper hundred dollar bills. It was a slam dunk case and Dr. Bill went to Federal Prison.

Chapter 17

PDA Forensics

G RANDPA MIKE HAD many people over the house since it was Garth's birthday. Aunt Mary called up a local bakery and had an ice cream cake delivered to the house." Everyone sang "Happy Birthday Garth." Grandpa Mike said, "Dr. Bill was in federal prison and I wonder if he will meet Robert Hannsen?" "Hannsen is that FBI guy who became a spy for the Russians and sold them so many documents." Double D, said, "Where did you learn about Hannsen?" Grandpa Mike said, "I saw this movie in 2007 called "Breach" "My favorite actor from the Bourne movie series, named Chris Cooper, played Robert Hannsen [1]."

Double D asked, "How did Hannsen get caught?" Grandpa Mike said, "The FBI got Hannsen to leave his PDA alone at the office, then they collected all the data using PDA forensic techniques." Double D said, "Do you think I could watch it?" Grandpa Mike said "I will set up the DVD on our TV for you."

Double D then watched the video and replayed the section where the PDA forensics was performed on Hannsen's PDA. Grandpa Mike said, "Double D, if you were going to do PDA forensics, "How would you do that?" "Double D said, "I would make sure I have written permission to have the PDA and then examine it." "That permission might be a signed policy if it was in a corporation and a search warrant if it was a public sector criminal case." "I would also make sure that the chain of custody form was updated as I examined the PDA." "If the PDA was still turned on when I got it, I would make sure that it was in a Faraday Bag so it did not connect to other computers or wireless devices."

Double D took another plate of ice cream cake and then said," I would next make sure that my examination machine was not connected to the Internet or any other devices." "I would disable the infrared ports, the Ethernet port, the Bluetooth, and wireless connections." "This way I am sure that nobody could connect to the examination machine and tamper with the evidence." "Then I would run antivirus software to make sure that no malware was on my examination machine."

Grandpa Mike said, "The preparation for an examination seems crucial or else someone can accuse the examiner of having the evidence tampered with." Double D agreed and said, "Then I would make sure that I can run the examination software and that the license was up to date for me to use." "Then I would use Paraben's Device Seizure or Guidance Software's Encase to collect the data." "The software has a write blocker built in so that I don't change evidence on the PDA and spoil the evidence." "Then I would select the correct cable for the PDA and connect it between the PDA and the examination machine." "Lastly I would follow the software wizards on the examination software and collect the evidence." "I would also add my name, address, organization, logo, and case details." "When I was done, the software would be used to generate a report that was ready for court."

Grandpa Mike said, "Double D, I feel as if I am ready to examine a PDA!" "Where can I read more about this subject?" Double D said, "It is also good to read books about Cybercrime that discuss both theory and real cases." "A good book to increase your knowledge in this new field is called, "Scene of the Cybercrime [1]." ""The book also discusses many fundamentals such as laws, policies, and then goes into some of the technical aspects of such crimes."

References

1. URL Accessed January 2, 2011 http://www.imdb.com/title/tt0401997/
2. Shinder, D., Cross, M., (2008), "Scene of the Cybercrime", Published by Syngress Books, 704 pp, ISBN 978-1597492768

Chapter 18

Denials of Service (DoS)

G RANDPA MIKE AND Aunt Mary were talking when Garth walked in. Aunt Mary said that she heard the neighbor's kids talking about a D-O-S. Grandpa Mike said, "DOS stands for disk operating system and it was loaded on 5.25 inch floppy disks into a disk drive." "Then you booted up." Garth said, "I doubt the kids were talking about such a museum topic such as that."

Double D came in the house and heard part of the conversion regarding computers and museum. Double D said," There is an excellent computer museum called the Infoage Museum in Wall, New Jersey [1]." "I went there with a colleague to see if I could borrow a very old machine for an investigation that I was doing on an eight inch floppy disk." "They also have a television and radio museum too."

Garth said, "I went there too one time." "They also had a giant satellite dish on Marconi Road." "It was part of Project Diana and the Search for Extra Terrestrial Intelligence (SETI) Project." Aunt Mary said, "I saw a movie about that topic called, "Contact." "It was in 1997 and had the character Dr. Elly Arroway played by actress Jodi Foster [2]."

Grandpa Mike said," We were talking about D-O-S and then you guys got into some kind of Roswell spaceman topics." Garth then said, "D-o-S can also mean a denial of service." "That is when people cannot use an online resource because it was made unavailable by someone." Aunt Mary said, "Someone could just cut the electrical powerline to a place with a webserver." Garth said, "Yes, they could also do that or a crime known as arson and just burn the place down."

Grandpa Mike said," I saw this fellow at the stationary store who said he had a denial of service to his email account because someone sent him 32,000 emails at once." Garth said, "That type of tool is called Quickfire and was used in an online component of a conflict between Palestine and Israel. [3]"

Garth got in front of everyone and said," A Denial of Service (DoS) can also be a result of a bot that you download on your computer." "The Gaobot is a piece of software that keeps your security software from working [4]." Gaobot also steals the registration on your installed software [4]."

Double D said, "A distributed denial of service or DDoS can also be the result of a Ping of Death." This is where thousands of computers or more receive a bot." "Then a botmaster gives a command that causes the drone computers to ping a server until it is overloaded with requests and then shuts down [5]."

Garth said that any type of methodology that makes a resource unavailable to a user is a denial of service. "Imagine that we have a database that sales people update daily." If we change the database so that it can be read, but not modified, it too is a form of denial of service."

Aunt Mary said, "Enough computer talk, let's see if there is some ice cream in the freezer!"

References

1. URL Accessed January 3, 2011 *www.infoage.org*
2. URL Accessed January 3, 2011 *http://www.imdb.com/title/tt0118884/*
3. URL Accessed January 3, 2011 *http://www.mail-archive.com/cybercrime-alerts@topica.com/msg00168.html*
4. Gralla, P., (2005), "PC Pest Control", O'Reilly Publishing, California, ISBN 0-596-00926-7, Page 258
5. Maiwald, E.,( ), "Network Security, A Beginner's Guide", Published by Osborne, a McGraw Hill company, ISBN 0-07-222957-8, pp 48-50

Chapter 19

Digital Camera Forensics

DOUBLE D GOT a call from Grandpa Mike and said that he lost some digital camera pictures from a birthday party at the house. Grandpa Mike also told Double D that a car was stolen across the street about the same time that the birthday party went on. Grandpa Mike said, "Aunt Mary sits by the front window and we took loads of pictures of her." "I think some of the pictures may also show the robbery taking place across the street." "The pictures could hold a key to the van's license plate that was partially identified by a man who was walking his dog nearby." "However; I do not want to bother the police unless I have some pictures that are useful to them."

Double D said, "Let me get my Tableau USB write blocker from the car and my software called Recover My Files." "Recover My Files is less than $100 USD and can be downloaded online [1]." "The software can be run and it will allow me to find any connected drives and missing files." "The Tableau USB write blocker is so that I do not change what is on your camera."

Grandpa Mike said, "I did not use the camera since I lost the pictures." Double D said, "Good, if you delete a picture, the pointer to it is deleted and not the picture." "The picture is there until the camera needs that available space and writes over it." "The pointer to the file is associated with the file allocation table that links the file table with the cluster where it can be found." "Clusters are made up of groups of 512 bytes." "Your camera uses a FAT 32 format which is the same file system used on that windows 98 desktop that Garth has downstairs."

Grandpa Mike said, "Let me microwave a bag of popcorn for you since this may take some time." Double D said, "a big part of computer forensics or digital camera forensics is just babysitting the technology while the tools run and recover data." Grandpa Mike said, "It sounds like the job I had at the guard agency where I just sat there and then called the police if someone broke in."

Double D connected a cable to the Tableau Write Blocker which was connected to the computer. Double D ran some antivirus software and verified that the examination computer was not connected by any means to any other network. Then he ran Recover My Files which found the camera. Then he selected the type of photos that he wished to recover. Then they ate the popcorn as the software went byte by byte and recovered the pictures.

When it was done, they recovered the pictures and burned them to a CD. The CD had about five pictures where parts of the carjacking could be seen. They decided to drive, with the CD, to the local police station and then create a report.

References

1. URL Accessed January 3, 2011 *http://www.recovermyfiles.com*

Chapter 20

Skimming Credit Cards at the Gas Station and Restaurant

GRANDPA MIKE DROVE the family to the Federal Prison to visit Dr. Bill. They stopped at the local gas station. It was what you call a mom and pop operation. It was not a regular franchise gas station such as Valero or Shell. A fellow got off his old rocking chair and approached the van. His blood hound lay on the ground and watched them. There was a car on cinder blocks in the yard too. The gas pump was so old and unique that Double D took a picture of it. It had a five gallon glass jug that held the gas and they could only sell five gallons at a time. This gas station was in a pine forest. It was along a road that was once paved but parts of it was broken and reverted to a clay sand mix.

The man said it is good you came here folks. The other newer gas station had a thief working there. He had this little box that he palmed in his hand and he used it to steal the information on the magnetic strip of your credit card. Grandpa Mike said, "How did he do that?" The gas station attendant said, "He had a small box about 1 inch by 1 inch by 3 inches and had a big crack in it where you slide a credit card through. Then the guy took your card and before he swiped it in the pump, he swiped it in this box when you were not looking. He was getting two hundred numbers a day this way and I heard he sold them to someone for two dollars a number. Then the attendant said, "We only take cash here."

Double D asked, "What did the guy who bought the two hundred credit card number do?" The attendant said, "I heard from this guy at the bar that he printed up the numbers on blank credit cards and then sold the credit cards for fifty dollars each." "He made ten thousand dollars." "I also heard that many people who bought the cards then bought gift certificates and gasoline and then disposed of the cards."

Grandpa Mike said, "Do you sell any food?" The attendant said, "We sell apple pie, cooked turnip greens, and some cookies." Grandpa Mike said, "I will take some cookies and I heard a story about some other credit card thieves." The attendant said, "Do tell." Grandpa Mike said, "I heard that there was this restaurant where the guy took your credit card and then when it was behind the counter by his machine, he took a picture of it, front and back." "Then the guy bought all kinds of stuff and had it sent to a house where the people were on vacation." "He used some fancy excuse so they did not question why the billing address and delivery addresses were different." The attendant said, "The cashier guy must have had someone on the inside in the credit card company because they would never go along with that." Grandpa Mike agreed.

Grandma Sally used the bathroom and then marveled at the gas station which seemed right out of a museum. She looked at the Western Electric 1912 candlestick telephone and said that she only remembered seeing these once in an old couple home. Everyone agreed that Cybercrime was probably not an issue for the people at the gas station, but it is for nearly everyone else.

The gas station attendant said to Double D and Grandma Sally, "If you have an interest in learning about antique phones and telecommunication equipment, then a good place to learn about them are from the Antique Telephone Collectors Association (ATCA) phone show or conference [1].

References

1. URL Accessed January 3, 2011 *http://atcaonline.com/*

Chapter 21

Cybercrime—Piracy of Software

GRANDPA MIKE CALLED up Double D and asked him to come over for Washington's Birthday. They decided to cook some traditional colonial foods such as pumpkin, turkey, and sweet potatoes. Grandpa Mike asked double D what software piracy was and how it was done. Double D said, "There are many people that use online websites to illegally sell and purchase or even share software that is not licensed to them." "This is piracy." "The software may be copied and mailed to someone or placed in a folder and downloaded by people who paid by many a variety of possible methods from: mailing cash, to depositing cash in an account, wiring money, or using some online payment service such as PayPal.

Aunt Mary was sitting on the couch listening to the conversation. She said," I also want to add that there is freeware too and that it is ok to share this software with others." "I got a program to edit my photos with freeware." "A friend of mine likes shareware programs too." "She can give me the software and I can use it, if I like it, I can send the creator of it a suggested donation."

Double D said, "Piracy is a crime because it deprives the software developers of a way of recovering costs and making a living." "It is theft." "If software developers cannot make a living at writing software, then their software business cannot survive and it will negatively impact commerce and communities."

Grandpa Mike said, "I learn a lot about technology and Cybercrime and software from listening to your conversations." "It is amazing how your conversations and vocabulary differ from generation to generation."

Chapter 22

Cyberterrorism

AUNT MARY WAS sitting on the couch and saw some news article about terrorism. She was watching television with Garth, Grandma Sally, Grandpa Mike, and some local Chinese friends to celebrate Chinese New Year. Aunt Mary asked, "Has anyone here ever heard of Cyberterrorism?" Mr. Lin said, "Cyberterrorism is terrorism done via the Internet." "If a group asked for money and you did not comply, they would shut down a sewer plant or cause an unplanned release of waste, that would be an example of Cyberterrorism." Aunt Mary said, "How could that happen?" Mr. Lin said, "Older SCADA control systems allowed managers to dial into water systems and control water or waste processes." "A good book to learn about SCADA is, "Cybersecurity for SCADA Systems [1]."

Aunt Mary said, "The same could probably be said about power plants." Mr. Lin said, "yes, if some group asked for money or else they would shut off the power." "That would be a form of cyberterrorism." Aunt Mary said, "I find it scary if some group could cause me to lose indoor light, television, computers, and microwave oven." "These are the things I use every day and I would be frightened if someone threatened my electricity."

Double D said, "Terrorism is done by scaring people and can be done with bombs or by disrupting their power and water." "It is my opinion that terrorism is for those groups who want to change a country's policy or course of action and do not want to get involved in the proper channels of politics to change things or cannot afford to have an open war with a professional army and navy."

Mr. Lin said, "I wish that people would learn to use the proper channels of politics and broadcasting to put their ideas in the public sphere and allow the marketplace of ideas to choose the best one." "I think people should look at the teachings of Jesus, Martin Luther King Jr., and the Buddha and embrace non-violence."

References

1. Shaw, W., (2006), "Cybersecurity for Scada Systems," Published by Penwell Corp.

Chapter 23

Talking to a College Administrator about Cybercrime

AUNT MARY'S FRIEND Rama was an academic dean at a college and asked how she was. Aunt Mary said she was fine and would love to see her. Dean Rama said she would come over to visit since school was closed for repairs and she had time.

Dean Rama came to visit and the two women caught up on old times. Dean Rama looked at the computer in the living room and said, "The computer is both a blessing and a curse in schools." Aunt Mary said, "I would love to hear your thoughts on it because I feel the same way with the computers at our home too. Dean Rama said, "The big thing I worry about is lawsuits." "There have been cases at schools where students do terrible things like spy on other students' sex lives with webcams or possibly other devices and then the person may commit suicide after being found out." "Then I worry about the parents suing the school because others feel school personnel can be everywhere on campus and prevent the misuse of such devices on our campus."

Aunt Mary said, "I worry about these social networking sites and Garth putting pictures of himself there drunk with underwear on his head and some new girlfriend on his arm." Dean Rama said, "I worry about our students doing the same and then applying for a job later." "These embarrassing pictures of people passed out from drinking and with lipstick art unknowingly drawn on their face often appear at the job interview after the company does a background search." "Many people think that once you take a picture down that it is gone but it is not." The Internet is archived and you can use the Way Back Machine on *www.archive.org* to find material that is no longer on the Internet but might have been posted as far back as 1996 [1]." "Then some parents want to sue us because they feel that we may not have adequately warned

51

their college children in the dorm about the dangers of posting online embarrassing pictures or did not stop their kids from posting these stories and pictures."

Dean Rama then said, "I also worry about the college kids who are downloading porn and some of the actors or actresses are below eighteen years of age, because it becomes illegal child porn." "Then it becomes a criminal case and if the story gets out, the bad publicity negatively impacts enrollment and alumni giving." "If I use software to stop porno, skin blockers and content blockers, then people complaint they cannot see any classic art with a penis, such as Michaelangelo's David."

Aunt Mary said, "This is a phenomena of avoiding adulthood, personal responsibility, and blaming others for our problems." I just read about it in a book by Diane West called Death of the Grown Up [2]." "It seems that in order to combat this culture, you have to have lawyers write excellent computer usage and Internet Usage policies, hold workshops, and do enough CYA activities to protect yourself and the college." "Then you need a big insurance policy too." "In the end you must raise tuition and then the same immature people complain about the increased tuition."

Dean Rama said, "The other problem that is a crime is too disgusting to mention and if it got in the public arena, would generate negative publicity." "The cleaning people found a public toilet spy cam and we just threw it away." "If we reported it, then it would be in the reports for college crime and be something the public media could pick up on." Aunt Mary said, "What kind of topic is that?" Dean Rama said, "The slang name is a potty cam and if you google it, there are 322,000 hits."

Dean Rama got up walked around and sat back down. She said, "There is that piece of American Federal legislation known as the Clery Act that we all have to comply with at school" "The **Jeanne Clery Disclosure of Campus Security Policy and Campus Crime Statistics Act**, codified at 20 USC 1092 (f) as a part of the Higher Education Act of 1965, is a federal law that requires colleges and universities to disclose certain timely and annual information about campus crime and security policies. [3]"

Aunt Mary said, "If I were going to be a college administrator, I would want to be one for an online college or university, a lot less headaches."

References

1. Way Back Machine, *www.archive.org*
2. West D., "The Death of the Grown-Up: How America's Arrested Development Is Bringing Down Western Civilization," St. Martin's Griffin; 1st edition (September 16, 2008), 978-0312340490
3. URL Accessed January 6, 2011 *http://www.securityoncampus.org/index.php?option=com_content&view=article&id=297%3Aclerysummary&catid=64%3Acleryact&Itemid=60*

Chapter 24

Ponzi Schemes

DEAN RAMA WAS enjoying her day talking to Aunt Mary. Then Garth came by with Grandpa Mike and Grandma Sally and sat down. Gath asked Dean Rama if some students received a letter in their email that if they paid ten dollars to the grand leader, then they could become a grand leader and collect ten dollars from others and thus be at the top of that pyramid.

Dean Rama said, "Many of my students get letters for pyramid schemes and some come with a warning that if you break the chain, bad luck will happen to you or your family." Some of my students come from places in the Pacific where black magic is still practiced and people are afraid of bad luck." They will sometimes engage in the practice unwillingly to avoid the possibility of bad luck.

Dean Rama laughed and said, "Pyramid schemes have been around for thousands of years but what is new is that they have been adapted for email and the Internet." Aunt Mary said, "It is amazing that dozens of generations have been fooled by the same scams."

Garth said, "I have heard of pyramid schemes but not Ponzi Schemes." Dean Rama said that in a Ponzi Scheme, named after Charles Ponzi, there is only one schemer who deals with everyone." "It is similar to a hub and a wagon wheel with many spokes." In a pyramid scheme, each new person is the top of a pyramid and directly benefits from members that they recruit after them. However; pyramids grow at such a mathematical exponential rate that they soon cannot last and then fail.

Dean Rama said, "The Madoff Ponzi Scheme was so successful because it paid out really high returns on investment and the investor's excitement and word of mouth help fuel its growth." "In that situation, the money from new investors is used to pay out earlier investors." "It is my opinion in most Ponzi schemes, the founder of the scheme tries to quietly disappear."

Aunt Mary said, "I believe that most of these scams that are successful are so because people react with greed and do not read the fine print." "The people who are scammed do not think the situation through or properly use their brains that God gave them." Dean Rama said, "We reap what we sow and if it sounds too good to be true, then it probably is."

Chapter 25

The Value of Conferences and Trade Shows to Learn about Cybercrime

GRANDPA MIKE WANTED to go out and eat. He then asked Aunt Mary, Dean Rama, Grandma Sally, Garth, Double D, and his old military buddy to go to an Indian restaurant for some spicy vegetarian cuisine. Grandpa Mike was trying to keep his cholesterol low and avoid more heart problems.

They got to the restaurant and ordered various vegetarian delights. Then Dean Rama said that it was good to go to trade shows to learn about the various products to help stop Cybercrime. Garth said, "What products could help stop Cybercrime?" Dean Rama said, "I went to the ISC East trade show in New York City one year and looked at some appliance firewalls." "These devices can be programmed rather easily to stop intrusions and inspect all packets that come into and leave your network." "I also looked at large enterprise firewalls which can be used at the college to guard many connections from hackers."

I also went to some Cybersecurity summits and various consortiums to speak to people. One of the fellows called Rami told me that he used to leave his computer on all the time. His wife left the old modem and dial up connection active also. She occasionally used an old dial up bulletin board service for information about disability. Rami then started to whine as he mentioned that a Trojan horse that got on his machine activated his dialer and modem and called up a foreign country and connected to an adult website. He said he later received a bill from his phone company for an additional three hundred dollars for that call." Dean Rama then found an article on that subject and saw that New York was preparing new laws against modem hijacking [1].

Dean Rama said, "One of the easiest things you can do to protect yourself is to turn off your computer and unplug the phone line when the unit will not be in use." "I would also suggest purchasing a firewall, antivirus software, and antispyware software, keeping it up to date, and then running these countermeasures often."

References

1. URL Accessed January 6, 2011 *http://www.cbsnews.com/ stories/2005/04/05/tech/main685656.shtml*

Chapter 26

Cyberbullying

D EAN RAMA SAID to the group at the Indian restaurant, "Do you remember that licorice candy that looked like medicine?" Garth said, "I do, it was one of my favorites." Dean Rama said, "Try this good anise seed dessert here." Garth said, "Anise seeds are said to help settle a stomach or belly ache." Everyone had the dessert and another round of tea. Then more discussions started.

Dean Rama said, "I am worried about Cyberbullying." Grandpa Mike said, "How do people do that?" Dean Rama said, "Some students take pictures with their camera phone and then email them to others along with nasty comments." "If a person is overweight and eating an ice cream cone, the comment will be something about her not needing that snack." "If a person rips their pants when tying a shoe, the picture and comments will be crueler."

Grandpa Mike said, "Is it just done my email?" Dean Rama said, "Cyberbullying is also done by SMS, texting, IM, and MMSing people." Grandpa Mike said, "What is MMSing?" Dean Rama said that MMS is for people with cell phones who send text and pictures from one phone number to another." "Email requires a separate email account."

Aunt Mary said, "How do people Cyberbully someone with only text?" Dean Rama said, "They may immediately text a person along with a picture and call attention to an embarrassing situation." Aunt Mary said, "it sounds like an telecommunication service can be misused for Cyberbullying."

Dean Rama said, "Perhaps teaching tolerance, compassion, charity, proper behavior, and respecting others can help greatly to stop Cyberbullying." "Then there are other technical methods such as not allowing students to use cellphones or wireless handheld devices unless it is for emergency." "Allowing unrestricted use of such devices in schools and allowing arrogant students complete privacy of their phones is a recipe for increased Cyberbullying."

Aunt Mary said," I feel parents should take an interest in their children's use of cell phones and wireless handheld devices and then teach them the correct behavior for such devices." "They should also tell them about digital forensics and what can be learned about how people abuse devices."

Chapter 27

Social Engineering, Pretexting, and Identity Theft

D OUBLE D DROVE everyone home from the Indian restaurant and then said it was a long day. Dean Rama said, that she just wanted to talk a little more before leaving. Aunt Mary said, "Dean Rama, I would just love to hear your thoughts on all this social engineering, pretexting, and identity theft that I often hear about in the news."

Dean Rama said, "You can just call me Rama, we are not at the university." Double D and Dean Rama did a Huntley-Brinkley style talk to Aunt Mary which is summed up below.

It is important to remember to cross cut shred important documents before disposing. There are people who steal garbage and then go through it. They may find a phone bill with various computer and internet account numbers. Then they may find other personal information and call up those places while pretending to be you. They may then order services they are unauthorized to or even commit identity theft. Identity theft is when people use your data to pretend that they are you and then get loans or services and let you get billed.

Social engineering is a real danger online or by phone too. People may collect information about you online and then call you up. Then they may pretend to be the head of security and ask for your username and password. The advice is not to give it to them. Once people have your email account, they can use it for spamming and perhaps selling counterfeit products that they do not want associated with themselves.

There is a website from the Department of Justice that discusses identity theft and how to protect against it [1]. One of the most important things is to guard one's personal information online or when disposing of papers. That means that you should be careful of the information you post online.

One should also avoid clicking on links from instant messaging and other emails because they often contain bots that collect your personal information and account information and send it to others.

References

1. URL Accessed January 7, 2011 *http://www.justice.gov/criminal/ fraud/websites/idtheft.html*

Chapter 28

Directional Antennas and Laptop Listening Devices

DOUBLE D WENT to visit Dr. Bill in prison and they were talking about the food and life in federal prison. Dr. Bill made a friend with a man Wally who was in prison for various Title 2 law violations for electronic eavesdropping and accessing computer networks that he was not authorized to. Dr. Bill then told Double D, "Some people have turned down the signal strength on their router." "The idea is that the network signal will not broadcast outside of the person's property and the people assume they are safe."

Double D asked how he connected to them. Dr. Bill said, "He considered purchasing the Cantenna but that is now illegal in parts of California so he did not want to get his name on a list [1]." "He then said that he built his own since there were many articles online that instructed one how to build your own directional antenna." "Wally built the device so easily, plugged it into the outlet, and then connected to various networks where he lived." "he got caught when he entered the police department network near his home." "They had his IP and Mac address in the log file and one day they caught him while connected."

Dr. Bill said, "Double D, there are every type of people in prison and every level of education including doctorates and lawyers." "There is no time off for good behavior in Federal prison and you must serve the whole sentence." "We also cannot have cell phones in prison but I heard that some people had them smuggled in and I can chance illegally using one for fifteen dollars a minute." "I also heard that some gang members still run the gang from prison and when they get out, they get a promotion in the gang."

Double D said, "The family will visit you next holiday." Dr. Bill said, "Time goes quite slow in prison and I await the visit."

References

1. URL Accessed Jan. 7, 2011 *http://edge.i-hacked.com/cantennas-are-now-illegal-in-ca*

Chapter 29

Bookmarked Sites, Saved Usernames and Passwords

AUNT MARY AND Dean Rama decided to have another lunch together. Grandpa Mike, Grandma Sally, Double D, and Garth decided to join them for lunch in the living room. Grandpa Mike set up some television trays and asked everyone what type of frozen dinner they wished to eat. Everyone made their choices and then dinner was served.

Grandpa Mike received a call from his old military buddy and put it on speakerphone since he did not feel like holding the telephone handset near his head. His buddy said, "I got a bill for all these books I supposedly bought online." Double D then said, "What do you think you did to bring this on or cause it to happen?" Grandpa Mike's buddy said, "Hey what do you mean by me causing the problem?" "I am the victim you unfeeling guy?" Double D said, "It did not happen to us, there must be a reason it happened to you."

The friend of Grandpa Mike thought for a while and said, "I sometimes carry a USB Drive in my pocket and when I pull my wallet out, it sometimes falls on the floor." "Recently I lost my USB drive." Double D said, "Did it have any information about your books?" The friend said, "No it did not have such information." Then I remember I got rid of my old desktop at the curb for garbage." Double D asked, "Did you save the username and password so you could quickly buy books?" Grandpa Mike's friend said, "That is it, I threw out the desktop and forgot to delete my book buying profile and my chat room profile too."

Double D said, "You better contact the people who run the chat room because someone could sign as you and improperly speak to children." The friend said, "I thought nobody would bother with such old computers from the mid 1990s but I was wrong."

Double D said, "Many people also lose cell phones or smart phones with Internet browser bookmarks on it." "This is a problem because dishonest people can use a lost phone to purchase items, access a person's home or work network, and make long distance calls."

Aunt Mary asked, "What is to prevent someone from claiming their phone was stolen and then purchasing many items and saying a thief bought them? Double D said, "That is fraud if you buy something and then try to deny the charge by claiming your phone was stolen."

Aunt Mary said, "A person could also get caught if they had an object in their home that was stolen. Double D said, "It is hard for a criminal to hide all the evidence of his or her misdeeds and something will show and give them away to a trained eye." "There are also temp files or parts of unallocated space on the hard drive that may have been used by virtual memory and have some evidence of transactions with the stolen goods [1]."

Double D said, "If you are interested in computer crime and how to investigate it, then Eoghan Casey's book and CD might be a good start for you [2]." "There is also a larger and newer version of the book that you may wish to read after that."

Dean Rama said," Double D, I really appreciate your suggested reading." "It has been good to see everyone but I must get back to the school." Everyone wished her well and then got on with their daily activities.

References

1. Nelson, B., Phillips, A., Enfinger., F. Steuart C., (2004) "Guide to Computer Forensics", Published by Thompson Learning, pp 410-412, ISBN 0-619-13120-9
2. Casey, E., "Digital Evidence and Computer Crime", (2000), Published by Academic Press, ISBN 012162885X

Chapter 30

Cyberethics and Laws Online

IT WAS SOME years later and Dr. Bill was released from prison. Garth, Aunt Mary, Grandpa Mike, Double D, Grandma Sally, Dean Rama, and Dr. Bill had a get together. Dr. Bill said, "While I was in prison, I read the Kindle Version of the Catholic Bible to learn about general ethics and God's Law [1]." "Then I read a book called "Cyberethics, Morality and Law in Cyberspace" to help me reconnect with right and wrong and the law in Cyberspace [2]." "I liked the book because it talked about modern issues such as free speech online and some of the limits which I learned was much further than I thought." "Surprisingly I learned that a book was published which included the source code for 14,000 viruses [3]." "I thought such a book would not be possible to publish without getting arrested."

Dr. Bill said, "Some of the chapters discuss the boundaries of intellectual property and one chapter demonstrates the borders through a battle between companies that have similar inventions such as the one click ordering."

Aunt Mary said," Dr. Bill, I am glad that you have been studying both modern and ancient sources discussing what is right, wrong and gray." "Dr. Bill said, prison is unpleasant and I do not want to go back."

References

1. God Inspired, "The Kindle Catholic Bible" Translated from the Latin Vulgate, Published by OSONOVA, Published in January 2010
2. Spinello, R., "Cyberethics, Morality and Law in Cyberspace," Published by Jones & Bartlett Learning, Ma., Fourth Edition, (2011), ISBN 978-0-7637-9511-5
3. " ", Page 191

Chapter 31

PDA Forensics and Wet PDAs

DOUBLE D HAD a case where someone dropped their PDA at a crime scene before fleeing. However; the bad news is that they sometimes get wet and this one fell in a puddle. Double D was over the house watching a football game with Aunt Mary and Dr. Bill and was talking about this wet PDA at the crime scene. Dr. Bill used to be very arrogant before prison but was much more humble since his release. He asked Double D, "How did you deal with the wet PDA?"

Double D got up and got a new box of shoes that Dr. Bill purchased. He took out a small bag of silica gel that was used to keep the leather shoes dry. He said, "I first put the PDA in a really warm sunny window and then let it dry." "Then I put it in a bag with silica gel crystals [1]." "The drying process took about four and a half hours."

Double D then said, "I did have access to Paraben's Device Seizure, I was able to replace the battery which had a pink dot and put a new one in." "Then I turned it on and then collected the data from it." "If there was any moisture left on the PDA and I turned it on, then it would have shorted out and my investigation would be ruined."

"Once I learned about the contacts, I was able to phone them and ask a few of them to come to the police station for questioning." "That was very important for the case." "One thing I learned to do when questioning people was to let people talk and really listen." "Sometimes I ask open ended questions and then let them tell me the important facts." "I also questioned then about inconsistent things they said and eventually they let me know they were lying with their body language." "I was eventually able to learn the truth."

Aunt Mary said, "I learned about the art of reading faces from a DVD [2]." "There are many personality traits that can be seen on a person's face." "The crow's feet around a person's eyes are actually empathy lines." "The ears being much lower than one's nose indicates a perfectionist."

"The DVD said that people with eyebrows close to the eyes and those with large irises and not much whites in their eyes like to demonstrate their feelings and are people who like to touch others." "Supposedly the art of reading faces goes as far back as ancient China."

References

1. URL Accessed January 9, 2011 *http://www.diylife.com/2011/01/03/ silica-gel-packets-unusual-uses/?icid=maing|aim|dl5|sec1_ lnk3|35281&a_dgi=aolshare_email*
2. "How to Read Faces, The Ultimate Advantage" DVD, Distributed by UFO TV, Venice CA.

Chapter 32

Real Products and Website with Great Prices but Used to Harvest Credit Card #s

DOUBLE D, AUNT Mary, Dean Rama, Grandpa Mike, Grandma Sally, and Garth went to an English Tea Room. They had Earl Grey Tea and some homemade pumpkin scones. Double D said that it reminded him of being in Hong Kong before the handover and going to a place by the Hong Kong Jockey Club. They had cucumber sandwiches and green tea back then and he had to see a detective about a case.

Dean Rama said, "It is amazing how the Internet has made the world seem so small." "We can video conference or talk with anyone at anytime in anyplace in the world." Double D said, "That is why it is important for security people and law enforcement personnel worldwide to belong to organizations such as FIRST, Forum for Incident Response and Security Teams [1] or the IACIS, International Association of Computer Investigative Specialists [2]." Double D said that it is also important for computer forensic specialists, sworn law enforcement officers, and various computer security people to take courses and learn about other people's cultures and study foreign languages." "If your area has many Albanians and Russians for example and they often phone or do Internet commerce with Russia and Albania, then you need to learn something about those languages so you can communicate with the immigrants in your jurisdiction." "Some people, especially senior citizens, may only speak their mother language and not English." "If they were ripped off online, you need to know for how much, and how serious it is so that you can dismiss it or get a translator and investigate in depth."

Dean Rama said, "I would like to change the conversation and discuss a local problem that occurred to one of my students at school." "I heard of a student who bought some things online at school from some website." "I believe it was a radio controlled airplane and wireless webcam." "It seemed as if it were a do it yourself UAV, unmanned aerial vehicle." "He never got the device and a friend of his who used the same website never got one either." "Then both men received charges of three thousand dollars which they never authorized."

Double D first thought about what Dean Rama said and then ate a custard tart. Then Double D said, "Some people create websites to harvest credit card numbers and then to steal them." "It is sad, because many of these people that are Cybercriminals have real e-commerce skills that could be utilized to make legitimate money if they were not so greedy."

Dean Rama said, "I also see a lot of misleading advertising online too." "I went to purchase a playset online for my nephew and upon close inspection, it only included the box." "It showed the contents of the box, but near the end of the ad, said it was only the box." Double D said, "If it seems too good to be true, then it probably is."

References

1. URL Accessed January 15, 2011 *http://www.first.org/*
2. URL Accessed January 15, 2011 *http://www.iacis.com/*

Chapter 33

Be Careful of Online Land Sales and Checking the Location

DOUBLE D, AUNT Mary, Dean Rama, Grandpa Mike, Grandma Sally, and Garth went to a Greek restaurant and ordered some grape leaves and Greek salads with some extra feta cheese. Grandma Sally said, "I would like to ask you about some funny online property experiences I had when I went on Garth's computer." Dean Rama said, "Do tell."

Grandma Sally told the group that she was looking for some dessert land online and found some online for about ten dollars per acre. Then she said, "I downloaded the picture and called Garth." "He looked at it and ran it through *www.gpsvisualizer.com* and the GPS coordinates embedded in the picture revealed that the land pictured was in Nevada, the most nuclear bombed place on earth." "I later spoke to someone online who was claiming to be part Shoshone Indian and found out there have been over 900 nuclear explosions in Nevada over a good part of the twentieth century."

Garth said, "Tell the group about the cemetery." Grandma Sally said, "I had someone call me up on my cell phone asking me if I would like to purchase a cemetery plot." "It was a strange call to get from a telemarketer." "I then went to the cemetery and met the salesman in the office." We looked at a map online at it had all the information about who was buried there and in what graves." "I said fine and bought a plot." "The salesman said the area I chose was in a closed part of the cemetery and would cost double." "I paid the extra fee, and he gave me the deed." "I asked to see the location section N, row 4, spot 51." We walked there and there was no such place." "Then I asked to go to the office again." "We chose another location that was vacant and walked to the plot." "I saw the spot existed and there was no nameplate or stone indicating the plot was vacant and existed." "I remember what President Reagan once said, "Trust but verify [1]." Double D said, "Land buyers of any type need to verify the land's location and also do a title search."

Grandma Sally said, "There was a chat room where someone told me that in Cebu in the Philippines, there was even some land bought that was under the sea [2]." Garth said, "Many years back before the Internet was even thought of, people bought underwater land in Florida."

References

1. URL Accessed 1/15/2011 *http://www.brainyquote.com/quotes/quotes/r/ronaldreag147717.html*
2. URL Accessed 1/15/2011 *http://balita.ph/2009/09/23/cebu-vice-guv-says-underwater-land-sale-contract-needs-to-be-rescinded/*

Chapter 34

Using VM to Investigate Malware and the New Environmental Sensitive Bots

D OUBLE D AND the rest of the family decided to go to an Indian restaurant and have Tandoori Chicken. Everyone went to the restaurant and then ordered a clay jar of Tandoori Chicken and rice with curry. The conversation and food was excellent.

Double D said, "I have to tell you about this situation that happened at work." "There was someone who clicked on an email attachment from a stranger." "Then they watched this funny movie clip and it took them to a website when they were done." "They closed the website and thought that was it." "Then the person had their bank call them about large withdrawals that were uncharacteristic of them." "Then their credit card company asked about taking a vacation in Bulgaria and making many purchases." "it seemed like a keylogger or rootkit of some sort."

Double D said, "I went to the guy's house and imaged the hard drive." "I copied the entire drive of both used and unused space." "Then I took the copies which were in a dd file format and made them a virtual file format." "Then I opened a window on my examination machine at work and ran his virtual file format." "It was like I had a window with his computer desktop running in it." "I could point and click on anything and run other software to see what was happening." "The bot that was running had a software sensor in it that knew it was running in a virtual environment and did not contact home." "Some of the new software is designed not to work in a virtual environment."

Aunt Mary said, "Cool stuff if you are Captain Kirk or some techno nerd!" Then the people at the table said it was interesting but too far out for them. Double D said, "Virtualization is good because you can have various windows on one computer and run a window with XP, another with Windows 98, and another with Windows 95." Grandpa

Mike said, "That VM sounds good." "We could keep the old operating systems and favorite programs but get rid of all that power hogging and space hogging equipment in the garage." Double D said, "I will set it up for you and then you can recycle the hardware."

Garth said, "I have certain video games and special hardware that only runs on certain operating systems." "Virtualization would allow me to have one convenient machine to play all the games." Double D said, "Virtualization will take the world by storm soon." Aunt Mary said, "Maybe I was a little harsh on the comment earlier." "Where could I get a book on desktop virtualization?" Double D, said, "Barnes and Noble online has a nice book called, "Mastering Microsoft Virtualization [1]."

References

1. Cerling, T, Buller, J., "Mastering Microsoft Virtualization", Published by John Wiley and Sons, ISBN 9780470449585

Chapter 35

The World's Oldest Profession
Goes Online

GRANDPA MIKE HAD everyone at the house for a Super bowl party. Everyone was discussing football and eating snacks. Then Grandpa Mike's old buddy showed up and was talking about how he was lonely and went online going through the personal ads. He was surprised to see the number of ads that appeared to be prostitution. Double D laughed and said," Pyramid schemes, fraud, and every other device have gone online, why not prostitution?" Grandpa Mike said, "Years back when newspapers got popular, there were some shady escort services that were thinly veiled prostitution services."

Aunt Mary said, "This is respectable suburbia, it is hard to believe so much Cybercrime can go on but then Cybercrime is done via the Internet and one cannot visibly see it." Double D said, "It does not matter if a neighborhood is rich or poor but Cybercrime can occur anywhere." "In fact the rich are more prone to Cybercrime since they have more to lose."

Double D said, "Today there is the sadness of online trafficking of people and using the Internet to shop for hookers." "There is now the e-brothel and I heard that people can look at girls from 30 different brothels online and get a delivery to your front step. "The author that discusses this further compares it to the convenience of ordering a pizza! [1]"

Aunt Mary said, "This convenience could spread disease, increase the wealth of organized crime, and cause a rift in families." Double D said, "There have been some allegations that people misuse Craigslist for non-existent products and for call girl services too [2]." "There is even talk that sex trafficking is increasing dramatically with the Internet and people can get specialty services too [3]."

Grandpa Mike said, "The Internet makes crime more accessible to everyone and the sad part is that people think they are anonymous and they are not." "People need to act responsibly on the net and not go into bad areas."

References

1. URL Accessed 1/15/2011 *http://www.shun2u.com/2010/01/online-brothel-e-brothel.html*
2. URL Accessed 1/15/2011 *http://www.ibls.com/internet_law_news_portal_view.aspx?id=1897&s=latestnews*
3. URL Accessed 1/15/2011 http://humantrafficking.change.org/blog/view/the_rise_of_the_e-brothel

Chapter 36

Cyber Bookie and Illegal Gambling Operation

G RANDMA SALLY HAD decided to have a lot of people over for Thanksgiving and invited so many people over. She had a few tables set up in the home and started the cooking three days before. The guests came over and started to sit down and eat. Dr. Bill and one of his former friends from prison arrived last and started the conversation since everyone was so quiet.

Dr. Bill's friend known as Bookie Bill said, "Anyone watch the Giants game?" Grandma Sally said, "I did and I lost a dollar on it to one of my friends." Bookie Bill laughed and said, "Grandma Sally, did you ever think of being the one who gets the dollar?" She said, "Well, I could use the money, whatever do you mean?" Bookie Bill said," When it comes to gambling or casinos, the house has the advantage and can always make some money." "Suppose you set up the roulette wheel and invite your friends over, you can let them gamble with pennies or nickels and you will have fin and make money if you are the house." "The other players will mostly lose and one or two will win some." Grandma Sally said, "I would not do that but my church often has casino night and they always make money."

Everyone watched and listened to the conversation with great delight. Garth said, "I could set up a real time roulette wheel in the basement with a high resolution webcam and take bets." Bookie Bill said, "You could do that and post results on a webpage or to a bulletin board service that people call in on." Grandma Sally said, "Garth you could make money that way but some sore loser would probably turn you in and you would get set up for a sting operation and arrested."

Dr. Bill said, "I met a guy in prison who was old and years back ran a gambling and sports betting operation by telephone." "Everything was written on dissolvable rice paper or magician's flash paper." "If law enforcement people came by, he would put the bets written on rice paper in the water in there was no trace of them." "If they were on flash paper, with one throw the papers went up in flames."

Dr. Bill said, "Listen, all this talk seems like old forms of gambling and very museum like." "Today people have a videogame like interface on a server and an automated shopping cart like any website uses." If it is not a licensed and legal casino, the server and phone support might be offshore in a country that has no extradition treaty with the United States and no Cybercrime laws."

Grandpa Mike said, "I may just google the term, "online gambling," download some software, and investigate this matter myself." Grandma Sally said, "I am pulling the plug on the computer and everyone better get back to Thanksgiving Dinner!"

Chapter 37

Cyber Harassment and Purchases

IT WAS STILL Thanksgiving and Double D said, "I got many enemies since I have arrested many people." "They can also find out my address since I coach baseball and am active in church." "Recently I had both men and women's pornographic magazines sent to my house and some sex products were sent to my neighbor's address with my name." Grandma Sally said, "One of your enemies probably used your name and address to order some porno magazines and you will get billed later." "Then a collection agency will come around after you do not pay." "If you pay all these magazines, you may get on some secret sex magazines mailing list which will be sold to others and produce more junk mail." "I suggest you tell your police chief, he probably dealt with this before and knows how to deal with it."

Garth said, "When I was a kid, my classmate got angry at me and tore out every post paid card in every magazine he could find." "He made up names such as Ben Dover, Seymour Butts, and Alonso Digrussy." "The postmaster called up my parents and said there was a harassment campaign against me." Grandma Sally laughed and said, "I remember that situation." "There were army recruiters calling, magazines arriving, and packages of strange items arriving as cash on delivery."

Double D said, "I worry about someone going in the chatrooms, pretending to be me, and then trying to meet boys or girls for sex." Grandma Sally said, "If there is a word of that, people will think you are a sex offender." "Even if you are investigated and cleared, people will think that they just could not find the proof and you are really guilty." "If you are mistakenly convicted, your credibility and career is gone." "Forget working with kids as a coach and the church has enough stories of offenders, let's not go there." "Talk to your chief right away!"

Double D said, "I remember that a student alleged that a principal was a pedophile and it disrupted school [1]." Grandma Sally said,

"Double D, my Grandma Nelson said that credibility was like virginity, once you lose it, you cannot get it back." Some people at the dinner tables laughed and others gasped at her remark.

References

1. URL Accessed 1/16/2011 *http://cyberbullying.us/blog/can-schools-discipline-students-for-creating-a-mean-facebook-page-about-a-teacher.html*

Chapter 38

Fear of Flying and Cybertherapy

DOUBLE D AND Aunt Mary were talking at Thanksgiving. Aunt Mary said, "I was invited to go to Malaysia by a friend to go to a bank and remove some things from a safe deposit box for her." "She will pay for my flight, hotel, and taxis." "I can even take two extra days to go sight-seeing and see the temples and beaches."

Double D went to get another leg of turkey and some vegetables. Aunt Mary said, "I want to go but I am afraid to fly." Double D said, "Can't you just get on the plane and sit for the 20 hours that it takes?" Aunt Mary said, "I might freak out and it will be worse because I am far from home."

Double D said that there were mental health professionals who used special computer tools and could help her. Aunt Mary said, "Please tell me more, I will do it." Double D said, "I once visited a place where they had airline seats set up in a formation that looked like an airplane." "Then they had these boards under the feet of those sitting there." "There were large speakers too and each person who sat there wore a head mounted display."

Aunt Mary said, "What else happened there?" Double D said, "There was a program that started and the shudders under people's feet shook as if they were on a real airplane." "Then they would see everything in the head mounted display that one would see if they were on a plane." "The sound of jets were on the speakers." "It was just like flying on an airplane with all the sights, sounds, and feels of a real flight." "Then the mental health professional operating the program can help the person get over their fears." "It is said to be effective and have a high success rate [1]."

Aunt Mary finished her turkey and stuffing and said, "Where could I learn more about this type of science that blends computer science and mental health?" Double D said, "I know what you are thinking,

81

you want to tell Dean Rama so that she can offer it at the school." Aunt Mary said, "You must be psychic Double D." Double D said, "Try the Cyberpsychology and Cybertherapy conference that takes place every June [2]."

References

1. Doherty, E., (2005), "Computer Recreation for Everyone", Published by Authorhouse, ISBN 9781420822397
2. URL Accessed 1/17/2011 *http://www.interactivemediainstitute. com/CT16/*

Chapter 39

Understanding IP Addressing, Subnetting, and Class A,B,C Networks

G ARTH WAS TALKING about logs with Aunt Mary since he was doing some part time tutoring. The young man said to Garth, "What is the Log_2 4096? Garth said it is just 2^X=4096. Aunt Mary said 2^1=2, 2^2=4, 2^3=8, 2^4=16, 2^5=32, 2^6=64, 2^7=128, 2^8=256, 2^9=512, 2^{10}=1024, 2^{11}=2048, so 2^{12}=4096, so the Log base 2 of 4096 = 12. We need to understand logs so we can talk about masks and sub netting. Aunt Mary said, "Speaking of logs, I remember a different kind of log." I remember the Carvel ice cream cake log that tasted so good."

Aunt Mary also said, "I remember another way to figure this out using the calculator." "The log (base 10 or common log) of 4096 divided by the log (base 10 or common log) of 2 = .36/.3 and that equals 12 too.

Garth said, "Aunt Mary, there are some protocols we need to discuss if we are going to have a serious talk on computers and networks." "A bit is a small charge or no charge." "It is a 1 or 0." "It is on or off." "Eight bits are a byte." "Everything on computers is stored in bytes." Digital pictures are made up of millions of bytes or megabytes." "If I say that a 2 MB JPG picture is traveling on a network, that means that a two million (approximately) byte picture in a JPG format is travelling on the network." Aunt Mary said, "Wait a minute, let me write that down."

After a couple minutes, Aunt Mary was ready to learn more and Garth started to talk about IP addresses. "There are IP 4 and IP 6." "Because of the billions of people worldwide who are joining the Internet, 4 sets of numbers are not enough." "Now we have IP 6 which has 6 sets of numbers." "The Number 135.23.45.9 is an example of an IP4 number." "The IP address is made up of four sets of number or octets, which means 32 bits." "Each network card in the computer has a unique MAC address too." "Sometimes log files contain a person's IP address and MAC address." "An example of a MAC address is C9-23-44-5F-11-13 and it is made up of 6 bytes or octets." "A MAC address is 6 octets of 8 bits which equals 48 bits." "The American Registry of Internet Numbers was started in 1997 and governs IP registration in the USA, some North Atlantic Islands, Canada, and the Carribean."

Aunt Mary said, "I overheard Garth talking about IP addresses and some examples of class A networks and then class B networks, and class C networks." "Do I have an IP address?" Double D said, "I have an IP address and so do you if you are connected to a computer network." "I opened up a DOS window in Windows XP and typed in IPCONFIG /ALL and hit the enter button." It showed my address as 192.168.1.101 and that showed that I am on a class C network." If the first set of numbers is 192 or higher, then it is a class C network." The subnet mask for a class C network is 255.255.255 and that means that the last set of numbers is for the class C network." "The last set of numbers is 8 bits and 2 to the 8th power is 256." "Then 256-2 reserved addresses is 254 address for people to use." Aunt Mary said," A class C license means that someone has 254 addresses to use and has a number that starts with 192 or greater and has a subnet such as 255.255.255." Double D said, "Wow, you understand."

Aunt Mary said, "Can I see what my IP address is and where it is on the map of the USA?" Double D said, "It is easy, just start up your Internet browser and type in the URL *www.whatismyipaddress.com* and it will show a map and your IP address. Aunt Mary said, "I am on a class C network with my little Linksys router and 253 other devices could be given an IP address at my home."

Double D then said, "If the first set of numbers is 128-191, this will be a class B network." "The subnet mask will be 255.255 and that will leave 2 octets for addresses." Aunt Mary said, there would be 16 bits (octet 1 and octet 2) to be used for addressing, 2 to the 16th-2 =65,534 addresses used for class B." "I guess that class B license would be for a big company."

Double D said, "If the IP number is 1-126 or less than 127, then it is a class A network." "That means that the subnet mask is 255.0.0.0 and that means that there is three sets of octets for addressing." "Two to the 24th power - 2 = 16,777,214 addresses free to assign." Aunt Mary said, "Class A networks are for big places like CNN world news."

Aunt Mary said, "It seems to me that you cannot really be an online detective unless you understand these principles that you explained." Double D said, "These are the fundamentals and you need to know it in case you have to go to court."

Garth and Aunt Mary were saying that the math tutoring is pretty good and it is easy to get $25 per hour. Aunt Mary said," I saw that online people can also tutor network security and computer classes or even stay home and become an online professor." "Wow, sounds great!" Double D said, "The network security teaching would keep my skills sharp and give me some extra holiday money for gifts." "By the way, you should remember that the high end address of any network or subnet is for broadcasting and the low end is for the system."

Aunt Mary said, "If I am going to make some money as an online tutor, I better brush up on my fundamentals." The seven layer OSI Model might be good for me to look at." Garth said, "Yes and learn about some of the standard formats out there for the Internet such as RFC 2026 put forth by the Internet Engineering Task force (IETF)."

Aunt Mary said, "I bought this new Ethernet cable by mail since I tripped and broke the old one." "It say IEEE 802.3 Ethernet group on some of the documentation." "Garth said, "The International Electrical and Electronic Engineers organization sets those standards and even decide on that RJ45 connecter as what is used with the computers." "That Ethernet is fast !" "Data travels at 100 mega bits per second!"

Aunt Mary said, "I have to call my friend Dean Rama and see how she is doing at the university." "We can talk about the TCP/IP model later."

Chapter 40

TCP/IP Model

AUNT MARY AND Garth were talking with Double D and Dean Rama. Everyone got together for some crumpets and tea. Dean Rama said, "The kids at school are amazingly smart." "We set up the network so kids in the dorm could not directly play network games with each other but they figured out if you set up a VPN tunnel from one room to another, you can beat our rules and play network first person shooter games like Doom." Double D said, "There are two ways to look at a network." "One way is by the OSI seven layer model." Garth said, "I hope one layer is the chocolate layer cake level, pass another crumpet." Garth said, "The other model or view of a network is the four layer TCP/IP model."

Garth said, The Application Layer in the TCP/IP is just like the OSI model's session, presentation and application layer. If I was looking at the videoconference program called Netmeeting, it would be at the application layer.

Aunt Mary looked at Garth's notes and said, "The Host to Host Layer in the TCP/IP model looks like the Transport Layer. That is the layer that retransmits TCP data and prepares the UDP packets of videoconferencing that are not retransmitted.

Garth said, "The Internet Layer is the layer responsible for sending packets of data across various types of networks." "These networks could be really different from one another so the data has to be encapsulated."

Aunt Mary then looked at the chart and said, "I see lastly that the Network Access Layer deals with the signaling and information travel over the cabling." Garth said, "that covers it and it is important that you know something about the networks where the data travels and how it gets there." "If you are going to understand Cybercrime, then you need to know a little of the technical details and not just the high level picture."

Garth said, "A good book for you to learn more about IP addresses, VPN services, and network services, is "IP A to Z" [1]."

References

1. Muller, N., "IP A to Z", Published by McGraw Hill in 2003,ISBN 0-07-141086-4

Chapter 41

Subnetting Calculations for a Network

DOUBLE D HAD won a thousand dollars playing the instant rub off lottery tickets. He went to the local convenience store and purchased a ticket. Then he used a dime to rub off the results. After he won, he mailed the ticket in and received a check for eight hundred dollars after taxes were withheld. He decided to have a party at Grandpa Mike's house.

The family had a party and sent out for pizzas and Chinese food. The pizzas arrived and everyone marveled at the thick crust, the oily cheese, the pepperoni, anchovies, green peppers, fried onions, and sausage slices. The doorbell rang again and Aunt Mary got up to answer it. She took the two large bags from the man and gave him a fifty dollar bill. She looked in the bag and saw Moo Shu Pancakes, Egg Fu Young, General Tso's Chicken, and Singapore Chow Mei Fun with shrimp. Everyone took a deep breath and just enjoyed the smell of good cooking. Then everyone had some food.

Double D started talking about work and subnets and how to calculate them. He told the group that he needed to set up a network for about 4094 people in town and had to get ARIN, The American Registry of Internet Numbering to assign an IP Address. It was greater than 256 people so he needed a Class B network. Then he needed to figure out the subnet mask, the IP subnet address, the first IP address, and the last IP address.

Dr. Bill said, "You know I was asleep in class that day and never learned subnetting." "Do you think you could explain it?" "I would really be grateful and it might help me get a part time teaching job in network security." Double D said," I would be happy to explain it if nobody has an objection." Nobody objected and everyone was just eating plate after plate of good food.

Double D said, "Let's make up an address for teaching purposes, suppose ARIN, through an Internet Service Provider (ISP), gives us 162.26.60.120." "I will give it the subnet mask 255.255.240.0." "So it looks like 162 and 26 is assigned by the ISP so we do not bother with it, so it gets the mask, 255.255." "Then 240 in binary is 11110000 because it is made up of a 128, 64, 32, 16, no 8, no 4, no 2, and no 1." "Please remember that 240=128+64+32+16."

Double D then had a piece of oily pizza with extra cheese, anchovies and hot peppers. He ate it with such gusto and then took a glass of water. He then said, "Now let us look at 60, that is 00111100 or no 128, no 64, a 32, a 16, a 8, a 4, no 2, and no 1."

162.26.60.120 don't care 00111100.01111000
255.255.240.0 don't care 11110000.00000000
Result = IP Subnet Address 0011000.000000000 = 162.26.48.0

Double D then said, the first subnet address is the IP Subnet address +1= 162.26.48.1 and the broadcast address is the highest address or 162.26.48.255.

Aunt Mary then said, "What is 255 in binary?" Double D said, "It is 11111111 or a 128, 64, 32, 16, 8,4,2,1 and add them up and you get 255." Then Double D said," The mask is /20=255.255.240. Garth said, "I think the /20 means 20 bits of value 1, all in a row." Double D said, "Correct 11111111.11111111.11110000.00000000 =/20 or 20 continuous ones."

Garth said, "Your notes are quite good Double D, I see that I can express this mathematically in an equation $/20 = 16+Log_2(65,536/4096)=16+Log_2(16)=16+4=20$.

Dr. Bill looked at some notes on his IPhone which he downloaded from the Internet. Dr. Bill said, "Double D, I believe your calculation means 4094 hosts." "What if people have wireless PDAs and smartphones they want to connect?" Double D said, "Hmm, first I must ask the general counsel if people are even allowed to connect such devices?"

Grandpa Mike said, "we have a lot of good food here." "I think it would be a good idea if we take a break from our computer studies and finish our meal."

Chapter 42

USB Cable and Malicious Software Driver

DOUBLE D AND Garth went to a local flea market and bought a USB cable for their phone and another for an external storage device. It was a very good buy. Then they were at the flea market and saw someone selling what appeared to be old versions of old Microsoft Office software with original COA. Garth said, "Why would someone purchase an old version of software like that brand new." One of the venders heard this and said, "You just have to register it and then purchase an upgrade from Microsoft for a really good price." "Then you will get the documentation and support." "Then both men saw a variety of designer products that just did not seem right. Before going home a man was selling some inexpensive laptops from a pallet that "fell off a truck."

Garth and Double D went to the house and saw Aunt Mary sitting on the couch watching television. Garth said, "I must show you this cable I bought at the flea market." "It usually costs thirty dollars but at the flea market it costs two dollars." Aunt Mary said, "Connect it with a storage device and see if it works."

Double D connected the cable and noticed that a window popped up and notified them it was downloading a driver. Double D and Garth did not recognize the website or driver that was downloaded but thought nothing of it. Soon afterwards Garth went to the online bookstore and bought a couple books for himself and something caught his eye before he clicked the order button. Garth noticed that he ordered his three books but there was also a refrigerator for eight hundred dollars plus shipping. Garth and Double D discussed the matter with Aunt Mary. Aunt Mary asked, "Did you accidentally click on something with a refrigerator?" Garth said, "I never even saw a refrigerator while I was online."

Double D, Aunt Mary, and Garth discussed the situation and realized this type of action never happened to them before. It seemed logical that it was a possibility that the cable had some embedded chip that triggered a response to download a driver from a website with malware software on it. The software driver seemed as if it took them to a website with a drive by download or perhaps gave them a poisoned software driver.

Double D said, "I could take the cable to work and connect it to a machine with a virtual environment." "Then I could see if the cable triggers a download of malware or causes a poisoned software driver to run." "The VM environment is perfect to analyze malware because the malware will run but not permanently damage the computer or change the software."

Aunt Mary said, "I found an article that said that some USB drives had malware on them [1]." Garth said, perhaps the cable sent us to a compromised website or caused us to download a driver with poor code." Aunt Mary said, "I remember in the old days in the 1980s when some people passed around copies of Lotus 1-2-3 and it had a virus embedded in it." "The virus was written in Lahore, Pakistan." "Two brothers allegedly distributed the Brain Virus on disks along with a version of Lotus 1-2-3 [2]. "Some people speculate that the motivation of putting the virus on the disks was to teach people not to illegally copy software."

Dr. Bill came over the house to visit. He then learned about the activities that had taken place and then assessed the situation. Dr. Bill said, "I remember the Brain Virus." "As a computer enthusiast, I examined the disks by putting them in the computer and then ran Norton Utilities' Disk Edit." "I remember seeing the address and telephone number of a place in Pakistan."

Grandpa Mike rang the doorbell with his pinky finger. Everyone came to the door and saw he had three pizza boxes. Then Grandpa Mike said, "I thought I would surprise everyone with some pizza for dinner." Everyone then ate dinner and put the computers conversations on hold.

References

1. URL Accessed January 24, 2011 *http://www.gadgetsnreviews.com/ our-usb-drivers-are-malware-ridden-says-ibm/1225.html*
2. URL Accessed January 24, 2011 *ftp://ciac.llnl.gov/pub/ciac/ sectools/pcvirus/goodwon.txt*

Chapter 43

Money Mules and Trojans that Gather Information for Cybercriminals

DR. BILL, DOUBLE D, Aunt Mary, Garth, Dean Rama, Grandma Sally, and Grandpa Mike had a small party to celebrate Dr. Bill's new job as an adjunct professor. Dr. Bill was the center of attention that day as everyone gave him cards, money, and an ice cream cake. Dr. Bill said that he heard from his friends who were in prison but now working from home.

Aunt Mary said, "I never told anyone before, but I once answered an Internet ad for a job to work at home and it was a disaster." "The company asked me to collect funds and move them to other accounts." "I did not get much information but I seemed to be a money mule." "I was also asked to purchase gift cards with account money and send them to people." "I also was told by someone that the people who received the hundred dollar gift cards were told to by something for about twenty dollars and send it to someone and they could spend the other eighty as they wished."

Dr. Bill said, "Aunt Mary, it was good that you kept your mouth shut and just walked away." "I also heard that computer criminals can misuse Trojans such as "Carberp" to go on people's computers to see what kind of security scanning software they are using." Double D said, "I saw a Symantec Security Website that said Carberp is a low level low risk Trojan that collects information on people's computers [1]."

Dr. Bill said, "I heard that Cybercriminals pay money for various malware programs to learn what kind of security programs people are using on their systems and to see if it is effective against organized crime's malware."

Aunt Mary asked, "Dr. Bill, why are there so many malware writers and Cybercriminals in the former Soviet Union." Dr. Bill said, "There are so many educated computer science people who are out of work and have families." "They need to eat, pay taxes, and feed their children." "Having morals is a luxury we have in the USA because we can always get some kind of job but what do you do when there is no work?"

Double D said, "There are all kinds of mules out there." "Some people are international diamond mules." "These mules take diamonds from mines in Africa and eat them." "Then they fly to the USA and take a bowel movement." "Someone collects the diamonds from the stool and then washes the diamonds." "The money is sometimes used to purchase guns and other types of arms." "These are called blood diamonds. [2]" "Aunt Mary said, "If you want to see a good movie about the arms trade and blood diamonds, just watch, "The Lord of War." "It is a movie with the actor Nicolas Cage." "I went to school with someone who worked for an international military aircraft company and they said it was a good representation of some people in that that trade."

Grandpa Mike said, "I think it is getting late and we need to get some sleep." As far as Dr. Bill, I am glad you got the computer teaching job." "As far as all these Trojans, it is important to have two security packages on your computer and keep these updated daily with all the latest antispyware, antivirus software, and firewalls." "I also believe that if a job sounds too questionable, get another one." "If you want to tell the FBI, go ahead." "Let's finish up our party and then go back to our rooms or home."

References

1. URL Accessed 1/26/2011 *http://www.symantec.com/security_response/writeup.jsp?docid=2010-101313-5632-99*
2. URL Accessed 1/26/2011 *http://www.ehow.com/about_5084710_definition-blood-diamonds.html*

Chapter 44

How Cybercrime has Matured, Cyber Extortion

DOUBLE D WENT to see Aunt Mary and Dean Rama at Grandpa Mike's house. Dean Rama was a little upset and wanted to see everyone." "She was in tears." Aunt Mary said, "I got your lovely card from Cypress and another one from Italy, what happened?" "You should be happy?" Dean Rama said, "It was a good vacation but then this fellow named Romeo Cassanova, if that is his real name." "He was so handsome." "I was sitting alone on the patio looking at the Mediterranean Sea and feeling the cool salt air." "This man and his friend sat across from me." "The man came over and sat with me and introduced himself as Romeo Cassanova, a direct descendent of the famous lover." "I was so lonely and smitten by his good looks and charm." "Then we went to my apartment and the next day he came to see me at the hotel cafe."

Aunt Mary said, "Sounds like fun, what is the problem?" Dean Rama said, "The man asked for three thousand dollars or else he would send everyone at the school, my friends, and relatives, a video of our night together." Aunt Mary said, "How did he do that?" Dean Rama said, "Romeo said that his partner got all her contacts via the unsecured Bluetooth connection from her phone." "Then when we went up to the room, he said that he put the cell phone camera on the mantle and did a video." Aunt Mary said, "Are you sure he had the contents?"

Dean Rama got up and walked around and then produced a report from him that had everyone in her phone book. She said, "It is so easy to get the information from your cell phone address book if you do not have the security features enabled and use a strong password." "I paid him the money but then he asked for more." Double D said, "I will contact some Europol people I know and see if I can help." "We can use you to catch him and maybe get your money back."

Double D got up and grabbed some coffee. Then he said, "I remember in the early 1990s, it was a big thing for hackers to break into a commerce site or military computers and get bragging rights." "They put in an electronic calling card or some type of code with their nickname." There was some intellectual pride in breaking some electronic border. [1]" "Now there are just small and large gangs of organized crime taking over the Internet crime and the super hackers who do things for bragging rights are a tiny part of the scene." "Many who were good at hacking now work for organized crime."

Aunt Mary said, "Let's think about what to do and then call it a day."

References

1. URL Accessed 1/26/2011 http://www.infosecurity-us.com/view/15412/first-decade-of-the-century-a-boon-for-cybercrime-says-mcafee/

Chapter 45

Social Networking Sites and Cyber Reputation Mismanagement

DOUBLE D SAID that he was talking to other digital forensic examiners and they said that they were reluctant to post questions on the forensic organization's website. Dean Rama asked why? Then Double D told her that defense lawyers and opposing forensic investigation companies download everyone's comments and archive them. Then they will print those questions out and use them against you in court to show that you do not know what you are doing. It is to reduce your credibility. He said that some people will even look you up on social networking websites and then friend your friends. They are not interested in being your friend's friend but wish to gather bad intelligence. For example, a person may friend your college roommate and then ask pictures where you were passed out on the floor with a six pack nearby and lipstick on your face.

Dean Rama asked, "How could that be, digital cameras were not invented then?" Double D said, "People often scan their own photos and post them online in a social networking website." Double D then told Aunt Mary and Dean Rama about someone else who even went to the trouble of making a fake social networking page as Bob Jones and put photo edited pictures of an investigator with some people at a brothel in Bangkok, Thailand. Dean Rama exclaimed that she was amazed at the ability and anonymity of people to use the Internet to slander others. Double D said it was easy to do. One has to just sit in a Cybercafe with a hood and sun glasses and use a new laptop that one paid cash for. If one has to sign up at the Cybercafe, just use a fake Identification Card or give a fake name and address.

Aunt Mary said that she was considering a way to make some extra money as a Cyber reputation manager and posting so many items that her client's bad comments were pushed far down the list or to a remote page. She was also considering finding out who ran websites and asking for negative comments to be removed for clients. Dean Rama said that reputation management was very good for people to make money and perhaps there could be a class in this in school for continuing education. "I believe that people who are pollsters, spin doctors, or have public relations firms would be great potential clients for such courses."

Double D also said that people can use digital cameras with optical zooms to obtain close up pictures of people and then they can use photo editors to cut the person out and put them in another picture. Then they could misuse a tool such as Picasa 3 and Google Earth to geocode the coordinates into the picture. He told them that he could take a distant photo of someone, cut them out of the photo, paste them into a photo in the Kremlin, and then geocode the coordinates in there. Dean Rama said, "How can we believe what we see and read?" "Perhaps even the reporters could be duped." "A person could even fake a picture such as WMDs in a country and start a war." Double D said, "That is why it is important to have digital forensic examiners who can read all the embedded EXIF metadata and investigate pictures." "It may not be worth the effort and expense to save one person's reputation but it would be worth it for an incident of National Security."

Aunt Mary said to the group that many people need to question what they read online and what the source is. She said, "I saw a video somewhere about HUMINT, also known as human intelligence." "There is what is known as poor intelligence which is hearsay from an unreliable source." "The same principles can be true with regard to digital evidence too and dubious or questionable digital evidence from blogs or possibly fake social networking pages should be discounted."

Double D's cell phone rang and then he excused himself from the group for five minutes. He listened intently, gasped, laughed, and then went back to the group. He then told the group how a friend of his named Bill was rejected for a job with the CIA based on his associations. Aunt Mary and Dean Rama said that they met Bill at a recent party and was surprised that he did not tell them that he was applying for the CIA." Double D said that at one time the CIA website discourages telling even your closest relatives that you are applying for a job there, or if it is done, it must be done with great discretion. The two women said, "We love a good drama and begged Double D to tell the story."

Double D said Bill applied online for a job at the agency and they gave him a polygraph test during the interview. They also checked out his friends, background, and employment history. It seems one of his close friends and students had a picture of the president of Cuba, Fidel Castro on his website and listed Fidel and Bill as friends. That website made Bill look like a friend of Cuban President Fidel Castro. Dean Rama asked how that could happen. Double D said that Bill's student posted a picture of someone who looked like Castro and was named F. Castro." Then the student posted some pictures of the real Fidel Castro and used a free online facial biometrics tool to see if the picture of F. Castro was the real Fidel Castro or a look alike." "It was part of a research experiment and not anything else."

Aunt Mary then said, "We have to not only watch our own activities but that of our friends in the digital world and periodically review the websites and social networking pages of our friends." Double D said that was correct and that all people in the world are said to be connected by six degrees of separation and began with a Hungarian author named Frigyes Karinthy [1]". Aunt Mary said that she once heard of a friend named Bruce at FDU who went to school with the Shah of Iran's daughter, so even I am only three degrees of separation from the Shah of Iran." Double D said, "I know you Aunt Mary so that makes me only four degrees of separation from the Shah of Iran." Dean Rama said that it is a small world and we must be aware of what we post and who we friend.

References

1. URL Accessed March 28, 2011 *http://empirelifecoaching.com/wp/ archives/77*

Chapter 46

Less Offenders Speeding and Knowing About Traffic Conditions

THERE WAS A small meeting at Dean Rama's home and everyone came over to see the new deck she had built off her kitchen. Double D came over and asked what the material was since it did not appear to be wood. Dean Rama told the crowd that it was a type of plastic that was made to look like wood and was guaranteed for fifty years. Aunt Mary, Double D, and Dr. Bill marveled at the material. Then a few cars sped by on the nearby road and slowed down in certain areas. Dean Rama said that it is odd but she never sees anyone pulled over for speeding.

Double D got in front of the group and said that he has not pulled anyone over for speeding in a long time and some of his friends who are patrolmen said that too. They wondered if people are more careful and observing the law or perhaps they know where the radar units and speed cameras are located. Aunt Mary said, "I don't drive, but I believe people from what I read, that motorists are driving slower because of the price of speeding tickets and the insurance surcharges that are later associated for such violations." Dean Rama said, "Good theoretical answer but I see people driving quickly and disagree with you." Double D then said to the group that he has another theory that perhaps people are letting others know where the speed traps are. Dr. Bill said that when he first started driving, people used human intelligence or HUMINT, and would flash lights at oncoming drivers to let them know of a trap. The group dismissed that idea after a discussion because nobody had seen that activity performed in many years.

Double D was looking through a magazine and suggested to the group that people could perhaps have a tool such as PhantomALERT. PhantomALERT is an application which may be downloaded and installed on a GPS device such as a Garmin, Tom Tom, Magellan, or on certain smart phones such as the Blackberry, iPhone, or Android [1]. Aunt Mary said, "I remember seeing an ad for PhantomALERT in the advertising section of either the Popular Mechanics or Popular Science advertising section in the back of the magazine." This application allowed people to know where speed traps, red light cameras, and DUI checkpoints were. The application was legal and also allowed people to access traffic cameras so they could see the traffic flow on highways that they were considering travelling on.

Double D said, "The GPS devices hold an amazing amount of data in them." Many inexpensive GPS devices such as the Garmin hold information on trips that people took and if paired with a cell phone, may hold data about hands free calls made or received in the car." "The advertising for PhantomALERT says that one can download the location of over 400,000 safety locations." "I was also amazed that the application will issue an audible and visual alert giving one time to slow down."

Dean Rama said, "The problem I see here is associated with the digital divide." "Educated people with a smart phone or GPS device and $9.95 for the application will be able to avoid tickets while the uneducated and poor will become vulnerable to tickets." Double D said, "The same thought could be applied to those who can afford excellent lawyers and those who are assigned a public defender." Dean Rama said, "Having disposable wealth appears to increase the quality of life in every aspect of daily living."

Dr. Bill said," The PhantomALERT application is good and could be of great service to emergency managers." "Imagine there is a toxic release plume in town and the officer needs to implement reverse 911 immediately, he could check the local highways' traffic cams and then give the townspeople the best evacuation route." "Every tool can be used or misused, a screw driver can be a burglar tool or it can be used to help pry a door and rescue someone from a burning car." "Tools or computer applications are not bad in themselves, it is how they are used or misused."

Double D paced around the deck and said, "You are correct, there are even Homeland Security applications for such an application." "If you know the location of traffic cameras and where police may be monitoring traffic, then you also know the roads that are not monitored and where a terrorist might use to avoid detection." Dean Rama said, "We live in an increasingly complicated world where there is sometimes a large gray area and not simple right and wrong."

References

1. URL accessed March 31,2011 *www.PhantomALERT.com*

Let's Sum it all Up

Dean Rama was talking in front of Double D, Aunt Mary, and the rest of the family at the Fourth of July Picnic. She hoisted a glass of lemonade and said, "This is to the Country and the Founding Fathers." Everyone lifted a glass and said, "To the Country." Dean Rama said, "Benjamin Franklin said that those who trade liberty for security get neither." Aunt Mary said, "I am not sure about national politics when it comes to computer networks, we give up a lot of liberty for security." "In the schools we limit what can be done on the computers and where we can go." Dean Rama said, "It is necessary to limit Cybercrime and predators on children."

Aunt Mary said, "Cybercrime can be broken up into: new crimes that use the Internet, and the same old crimes that are on the Internet." "There are pyramid schemes, online prostitution, lottery scams, etc. and then there is hacking servers, identity theft, and various fraud techniques that are only possible with the Internet. Dean Rama said, "There is great truth in what you say but also do not forget the terrorist threat and the Internet." "There is Cyber-Jihad and websites that recruit people to terrorism and then the terrorists can use online guest books, blogs, and email to communicate with." Double D chimed in, "Don't forget the petty crime such as selling the same iPhone three times to three different people."

Grandpa Mike said, "I learn so much listening to all of you." "When it comes to safety, I do many of the basic things you tell me too." "I have Norton 360 and keep the antivirus, antispyware, and firewalls up to date and running on my computer." "I keep the computer and router turned off when not in use." "I also use a wire and turned off my wireless capability since I don't need it." "I told my son and all my friends not to believe a Nigerian Prince is going to put one million dollars in my bank account if I give him my number and not to get happy about winning the Canadian lottery when I never even bought a ticket." "If someone contacts me on the phone and I am not sure if it is real, I have a sound effect on my computer that simulates my doorbell and I ask for their phone number and name so I can call back later."

Dr. Bill said, "I also reduce Cybercrime by not visiting all these adult websites, not downloading strange videos and programs, and by using a webmail interface to open email attachments from people that I do not know." "As a teacher, I have to open every email since I often get emails from potential students who also send their resume for evaluation to our programs." "I also tell students that they should not purchase things from unknown websites unless they first call on the telephone and verify some basics about the vendor."

Grandma Sally stood up and then grilled some squash and corn dogs on sticks for everyone in the group. She then said, "I have learned a lot about computers these last few years from all of you." "They enable people to communicate, perform work, and go to school from long distances." "They allow homebound people to purchase items they cannot easily get without a car." "Computers allow me and Grandpa Mike to anonymously communicate in forums online about serious subjects and not be dismissed by younger people who often practice ageism." "However; computers also allow others into my home to steal information or separate me from my money if I am not careful." "They must be used with care and some security must be practiced." "We are letting the world into our home when we connect to the information superhighway." "Just as we screen visitors to our home with a peephole at the door, on the computer we must screen our visitors with antivirus software, antispyware software, firewalls, and ask the correct questions by email before we move forward."

Dean Rama said, "You must use caution and be observant about your computer system that connects to the Internet." "It is important to also get the latest security updates for your operating system, browser, anti-virus, anti-spyware, and firewall." "Lastly, use common sense and ask other people you trust about things on the Internet if you are not sure."

Aunt Mary said, "This has been another great get together and I think we should put everything away and meet later to see the fireworks, Goodbye and God Bless."